Introduction to the Art of Stage Management

Online resources to accompany this book are available at: https://bloomsbury.com/introduction-to-the-art-of-stage-management-9781474257213/. Please type the URL into your web browser and follow the instructions to access the Companion Website. If you experience any problems, please contact Bloomsbury at: contact@bloomsbury.com

INTRODUCTIONS TO THEATRE

SERIES EDITOR:
JIM VOLZ, CALIFORNIA STATE UNIVERSITY, FULLERTON, USA

This series of textbooks provides a practical introduction to core areas of theatre and performance and has been designed to support semester teaching plans. Each book offers case studies and international examples of practice and will equip undergraduate students and emerging theatre professionals with the understanding and skills necessary to succeed—whether in study or in the entertainment industry.

Directing Professionally: A Practical Guide to Developing a Successful
Career in Today's Theatre
Kent Thompson
ISBN 9781474288767

Introduction to Arts Management
Jim Volz
ISBN 9781474239783

Introduction to the Art of Stage Management

A Practical Guide to Working in the Theatre and Beyond

Michael Vitale

methuen | drama
LONDON • NEW YORK • OXFORD • NEW DELHI • SYDNEY

METHUEN DRAMA
Bloomsbury Publishing Plc
50 Bedford Square, London, WC1B 3DP, UK
1385 Broadway, New York, NY 10018, USA

BLOOMSBURY, METHUEN DRAMA and the Methuen
Drama logo are trademarks of Bloomsbury Publishing Plc

First published in Great Britain 2019

Series design by Liron Gilenberg
Cover image: *Krabat* at the opera house in Stuttgart, Germany, 21 March 2013
(© Stuttgarter Ballett/dpa picture alliance/Alamy Stock Photo)

A catalogue record for this book is available from the British Library.

A catalog record for this book is available from the Library of Congress.

ISBN: HB: 978-1-4742-5719-0
        PB: 978-1-4742-5720-6
      ePDF: 978-1-4742-5722-0
     eBook: 978-1-4742-5721-3

Series: Introductions to Theatre

Typeset by Integra Software Services Pvt. Ltd.
Printed and bound in Great Britain

To find out more about our authors and books visit www.bloomsbury.com
and sign up for our newsletters.

For the Stage Managers who do the job
for the love of the work and not the glory of the spotlight …

Contents

Acknowledgments

Jim Volz, Debra Garcia Lockwood, Meredith Greenburg, Barbara Donner, Lyla Forlani, Whitney McAnally, Taylor Comen, Kelvin Vu, Ann Sheffield, Lee Helms, Jeffrey Wallace, Kelley Kirkpatrick, Kirsten Parker, Young Ji, Jill Barnes, John Holly, Evelyn Carol Case, Shannon Bicknell, Matthew Jackson, Joel Veenstra, Brian Grohl, Steve Linder, Meghan Umber, Kristopher Lythgoe, Rebecca Baeling-Lythgoe, Renee Duron, Lindsay Lowy, Patrice Lozano, Terry Cook, Graham Michael, and Rita Santos.

I would also like to offer special thanks to Kimberly Mitchell, without whose expertise sections of this text would not have been possible.

About the Author

Michael Vitale is a stage manager, production manager, and educator. He has many years of experience as an AEA and AGMA stage manager working in theatre, dance, musical theatre, special events, opera, and classical music. During this time, Michael has worked with companies across the performing arts spectrum in venues from the Hollywood Bowl to the Barbican Centre in London. Alongside stage managing, Michael spent time as an adjunct professor, teaching stage management at California State University–Fullerton and Pomona College. In 2015, Michael took a full-time position with the Los Angeles Philharmonic where, as a production manager, he now calls on the diversity of his theatrical experience to produce projects that combine disciplines in challenging and innovative ways. Michael holds a bachelor of arts in theatrical production from California State University–Fullerton, and a master of fine arts from the University of California–Irvine.

Introduction

Stage Managers are the lynchpin of any production. It does not matter if you are working in theatre, opera, dance, theme parks, cruise ships, special events, or any other performing arts arena. Stage Managers are the ones who keep the trains running on time and the people on stage safe. It is one of the most rewarding and difficult jobs you can find, and it takes a very special breed of person to do it well. The key to understanding the role of the Stage Manager, in any discipline, is understanding how diverse and disparate all of the other areas around them are. Each show has a large number of artists who come together from different backgrounds, with different specialties, and are asked to build something cohesive and put it on stage. That alone is a big ask. The director assumes responsibility for providing creative leadership to this group, but it is the Stage Manager who fills in the gaps and keeps the project moving forward.

One of the truly unique things about Stage Managers is that there is very little consistency in how people come to be a Stage Manager. Every Stage Manager has a very personal story of how they chose stage management as their career path. It is a discipline that has very limited visibility in pop culture or general notoriety, so many people don't even know that the job exists. That personal journey impacts the way that they will approach a job that varies dramatically from show to show, company to company, and discipline to discipline. The contents of this book have been built based on the personal experiences of Stage Managers who have done the job. The goal in writing it is to create a text that fills in some of the gaps that exist in the Stage Manager canon and hopefully provide a useful tool for new and seasoned Stage Managers alike. There is no telling where your career path will take you, and this book can serve as a resource to those who find themselves suddenly working in a world they never expected.

I have had the great fortune to work at the highest level of the profession I love. Working at the Hollywood Bowl or the Barbican; doing shows with my artistic heroes and giants of the field; being employed by companies I was in awe of, were always goals of mine—I just never thought that stage management would be the way I would get there. By way of introduction, I will discuss my own journey to stage management. Like many people who now work in the field of theatrical production, I began my interest in the performing arts as a performer. Part of this was my love of movies and my desire to act, and part of it was that performers are, obviously, the most visible people in any production. I knew that I wanted to work in that world and, as a child, the only job I could see was being an actor.

Soon, however, I began to take notice of everything else that went into making a show happen. I started to dabble in lighting, sound, and set design. I started to take a more integral role on each production, gobbling up as much responsibility as I could until my theatre teacher started to refer to me as the Stage Manager. I did not really understand what that term meant, other than it gave me greater access to explore all the different avenues working in a theatre could provide for me.

In my undergraduate theatre years I quickly became a theatre education major, as the coursework involved in that degree encompassed every possible part of the theatrical spectrum, including stage management. I truly began stage managing in college. It was the first point when I understood what the job actually was and I was able to determine if this was something I wanted to do or not. I quickly moved from stage managing theatre to being hired to work on special events for the university. These opportunities to work on nontraditional shows formed my approach to stage management. I began to embrace the idea that the Stage Manager needs to be flexible, that it wasn't always about being prepared but, rather, being prepared *enough* that you can pivot and change your approach at the drop of a hat. It also provided the chance to work with a wide array of people from many backgrounds, and not solely my peers.

I was very fortunate that those jobs in special events parlayed themselves into higher-profile gigs, which in turn introduced me to other large companies, and through that process I was able to build a career as a freelancer. That career included credits in theatre, opera, dance, special events, education, theatre for young audiences, and classical music. The wide array of projects that I have had the pleasure to work on spurred my interest in looking at other disciplines and industries that Stage Managers can work in. The biggest hurdle that I had to leap as I moved from gig to gig was that I had never worked in most of the disciplines I was being hired to do shows for. As a result, I was constantly dealing with a very steep learning curve wishing that I had resources that could provide at least some context for what I was stepping into.

Stage management education is, by and large, taught with theatre as the foundation. This makes sense, as most classes in stage management are taught by theatre departments versus music or dance departments. However, if the class does not branch out beyond the structure, culture, and methodology of the theatrical process, the Stage Managers coming out of the program will find themselves, like me, a bit at sea when stepping into any discipline that is not theatre. The same can be said of Stage Managers whose careers have only led them to work in the theatre. The idea of stepping into opera or onto a cruise ship can seem daunting if they have no frame of reference for what to expect.

That knowledge gap is what this book endeavors to fill. The goal here is to provide a practical resource for new and established Stage Managers. Not every chapter is going to be applicable to every person, but if you have been asked to work on an opera you can skip to that chapter and get a sense of how it differs from theatre and what to expect when you walk in the door. If you are a brand-new Stage Manager, the early chapters will take you through the process from beginning to end, using theatre as the model and branching out from there. The other element that will serve as a through-line in the text, and should be taken note of, is the concept of self-assessment.

This will be discussed in greater detail at various points in the text, but it is worth touching on here. stage management is, by its nature, a learn-by-doing profession. There is only so much you can gain from a lecture or reading a book, so you have to get out into the world and do it. The only way to grow your skills and get better at the job is through self-assessment. Taking the time to evaluate which things are working and which are not will help craft the kind of Stage Manager you become. Just as each director, designer, actor, and writer has their own unique style and voice, so too does the Stage Manager. That voice can only be discovered through understanding how your actions impact those around them.

For those willing to take on the challenge, stage management can be one of the most rewarding professions in the theatre. Though it can be stressful and exhausting, it offers the opportunity to be at the center of the action. Unlike any other role in the arts, the Stage Manager gets to walk the line between artist and technician, and leap back and forth between both. As a result, Stage Managers get to develop incredible relationships with everyone involved in a production and those relationships can last a lifetime. It is my hope that this text will provide an accurate and honest depiction of stage management today. Whether you are a new student or a seasoned professional, this text will hopefully bring something new to the table and be a resource for you as your career moves forward.

1

Role of the Stage Manager

Everyone comes to stage management in their own way. Many (most even) begin as performers: actors, dancers, musicians, etc. There are those who begin as designers, stage hands, or even directors and slowly find their way to stage management. The one thing very rarely heard is that someone always wanted to be a Stage Manager. The primary reason for this is that stage management is one of the most ill-defined positions in the entertainment industry. The fact that it is so amorphous has a tendency to keep it from gaining the kind of mainstream awareness that other roles in the theatre have, and so young people exploring the theatre for the first time do not realize that it is an option that they can pursue. It is not until they are working in theatre, in another capacity, that they see the Stage Manager even exists. It is fairly easy to identify the basic things that a Stage Manager does but zeroing in on a specific definition for what a Stage Manager is becomes more complicated.

Broadly, a Stage Manager is defined as the member of the production team who works directly with the cast, production, and creative teams to oversee the day-to-day execution of a theatrical presentation, with a special emphasis on the technical side of the production. I specify "broadly" because while stage management has certain key tasks that are associated with the job, the definition of what a Stage Manager's role actually is varies depending on the situation in which they are working. The phrase "it depends" comes up quite frequently when discussing the role of the Stage Manager and that is because the variability of the job, even within a single theatrical discipline, is so dramatic.

Understanding the basic functions of the Stage Manager in a theatrical process is going to build the foundation to do the one thing every Stage Manager needs to be able to do: adapt. Adaptability is the single most important character trait in a Stage Manager. Being boxed into a very specific definition of the role is how Stage Managers limit their viability in the workplace. The phrase "everything to everyone" is often brought up when people discuss the role of the Stage Manager. Every show is different, as is every cast and every creative team, so Stage Managers have to be able to adapt to the environment that they are walking into.

Who's who

"Stage Manager" functions as both a specific job title as well as a broad name for everyone working on the stage management team. Each member of the team is a Stage Manager but only one is *the* Stage Manager. The rest of the team have their own individual titles and responsibilities. The division of labor among the team is fairly consistent across theatrical disciplines but there are variations, particularly country to country.

Production Stage Manager

The *Production Stage Manager*, or PSM, is the lead Stage Manager on a show. This term is most commonly utilized in the United States and refers to the person who has ultimate responsibility for the stage management team. PSMs are normally found on large shows. It is not a requirement for all shows to have a (formally titled) PSM, and some companies steer clear of the term. Depending on the type of show, the PSM will handle payroll, scheduling of staff, crew administration, and trucking, all in addition to the standard responsibilities of calling the show, working with the creative team, overseeing rehearsal schedules, etc. The title also sometimes appears as a way to differentiate who the lead Stage Manager is on the show, even if they are not absorbing these additional administrative duties. As is clear, the usage of the term is flexible and really comes down to company preference rather than professional standard.

Stage Manager

The term *Stage Manager*, or SM, is used in two ways, interchangeably. The first is very general. "Stage Manager" can refer to any member of the stage management staff on a given show. It is used to indicate the department they belong to, in the way they might say "I am an electrician" when, more specifically, they are going to be running a spotlight. When "Stage Manager" is used in this way it is important to be very clear that it is being used generally. This is because its other usage is the specific title of one of the, if not the lead Stage Manager on a show. Whenever the title Production Stage Manager is not used the lead Stage Manager is referred to simply as the Stage Manager. This seems a little convoluted but makes a lot of sense in practice. Either way, the Stage Manager is responsible for serving as the chief liaison between the creative team, production team, and crew. They will oversee the schedule, organize the backstage, and be ultimately responsible for the smooth running of the show, both in rehearsal and performance. The Stage Manager will also be charged with calling the show. *Calling the show*, which will be discussed in depth later, refers to the calling of all technical cues in performance. These include lighting changes, scenery moves, projection, sound, etc. By calling the show, the Stage Manager holds most of the power in how a performance will progress.

Assistant Stage Manager

The *Assistant Stage Manager*, or ASM, serves as the "boots-on-the-ground" member of the stage management team. There is often more than one ASM on any given show to ensure that the physical running of the show goes without a hitch. The specific responsibilities of the ASMs change from discipline to discipline and from show to show, but across the board they are actively responsible for the physical execution of everything that happens on the stage. While the Stage Manager is locked in a booth or tucked away in a corner, calling the show, the ASMs are ensuring that cast are in the correct locations, quick changes are going well, props are preset, scenery is ready to move, etc. The title "Assistant Stage Manager" is a bit of a misnomer as the ASM does not really assist the Stage Manager. They have their own set of responsibilities on the show and serve as a compliment and partner to the lead. Every SM/ASM relationship is going to be different and some SMs will treat their ASMs as assistants, but this is not the norm and should not be the goal. A good Stage Manager acknowledges the need for a strong team dynamic and will give autonomy to the ASMs to do their job correctly. The role of ASM is fairly consistent across disciplines, shows, and countries.

Deputy Stage Manager

The *Deputy Stage Manager*, or DSM, is a role that is almost exclusive to the UK. The DSM falls somewhere in between the SM and ASM in their duties. The most significant difference in this role is that while the DSM is not the lead Stage Manager, they are responsible for calling the show. This is a substantial deviation from the structure previously discussed but makes a lot of sense. By having someone designated as the show caller in both tech and performance, the lead Stage Manager is free to put out fires and help to make critical decisions with a clear headspace. One of the challenges of being the PSM or SM is that you are asked to keep the show running while simultaneously being responsible for making on-the-spot decisions when things go wrong. With the UK structure, the DSM can remain focused on calling a clean show, while the Company Stage Manager is free to address concerns and jump in when needed.

Company Stage Manager

The *Company Stage Manager*, or CSM, is the lead Stage Manager in the UK structure. The CSM is a hybrid of the Production Stage Manager and a Company Manager. In addition to the administrative duties related to the crew and stage management staff, the CSM will also oversee the management of the cast. This can include tracking payments, ensuring riders are adhered to, managing publicity schedules, etc. They will also retain the responsibility for the production as a whole. By removing certain rehearsal and calling duties from their plate, the CSM is able to assume this more administrative role as they will be more available to everyone in the company. That being said, the CSM will still continue to support the onstage activities by calling certain performances to give the DSM a break, or providing back up to the ASMs in the event they need an additional pair of hands.

Assembling the team

Putting together a stage management team is a daunting process. Some are assembled solely by the producer, while others are put together based on the Stage Manager's preferences. Either way, the same basic issues need to be carefully considered before offering people the job. It is important to put together a well-balanced team that will first and foremost serve the production. There are two key questions that will help you get to that balanced team:

1 **What is their background?**

    It is important to consider what each team member can bring to the table, in terms of knowledge base. Sometimes this has to do with technical experience and other times it is related to personal interests. For example, if a show is going to be using automation and the Stage Manager has never worked with it before, it would make sense to bring on an ASM who has. By adding this knowledge base to their team the Stage Manager now has a resource they can rely on backstage. Trying to balance the team with people who can fill in gaps is important for the success of any stage management team. It is critical to not have an ego about bringing people on who know more than you. In fact, it should only make the Stage Manager more confident, as they have someone they can truly rely on in their corner.

2 **How does their personality fit in?**

    Any hiring of an employee is going to be full of subjective landmines. There is no empirical way to hire someone while removing bias from the equation. In the case of hiring Stage Managers, the subjective approach is an asset. The reality is that at least 85 percent of a Stage Manager's job is dealing with people. This means that the personality of the individual is a critical concern and should be an important factor in how a stage management team is assembled. Consideration should be given to the creative team that the Stage Managers will be working with and the tone and tenor of their approach to the work. If the creative team is comprised of very serious, stoic, or straight-laced people, the stage management team needs to be able to slip into that environment comfortably. Putting Stage Managers who are gregarious, jovial, or too relaxed in that environment has the potential to cause friction and discontent on all sides. The reverse is also true. Putting Stage Managers who are overly serious and do not know how to have a good time in a room with a director who approaches the work as play can be equally problematic. It is up to the person who is doing the hiring to try to get a read on all the personalities and try to build a team that will balance well all around.

Artist v. technician

One of the fundamental questions you must ask yourself as a Stage Manager is "am I an artist or a technician?" This may seem an irrelevant topic but, in a constantly changing field like stage management, how you view yourself greatly impacts how you approach the work and how others view you. Before getting into the argument for each of these identifiers, it is important to note that every Stage Manager is going to be some combination of both of these.

The argument for technician

Obviously, there is a significant amount of technical knowledge, or at least comfort with the technical side of theatrical production needed to be a Stage Manager. There are many Stage Managers who very specifically self-identify as technicians. This usually means that they divorce themselves from the artistic discussions involved in mounting a show. They view their responsibilities in the process as revolving around executing the artistic vision rather than participating in it. To some extent, this way of thinking does make sense. As a Stage Manager you are not always going to be permitted to have artistic input on a project, and your job, in its most basic form, is the implementation and maintenance of the artistic product of the designers and director. Removing your own artistic sensibilities from the equation can make it easier to more accurately replicate the work of others, as you won't be combatting your own personal tastes.

Some people self-identify as technicians simply because that is where their interest lies. Everyone comes to stage management in a different way and if an individual never had an interest in nontechnical disciplines, or they just found their passion lies in the technical side, honoring that is important. There are jobs out there that are even geared towards Stage Managers who see themselves more as technical supervisors than someone who straddles the creative and production teams. The trick is just finding the right job that satisfies your personal desires for your work life.

The argument for artist

A significant element of the role of the Stage Manager is the collaboration with the members of the creative team (designers and directors). This collaboration can require a level of artistic understanding and discourse that makes the Stage Manager feel like a part of the creative team itself. Viewing themselves as an artist can help support this collaboration. Viewing themselves as an artist can also support the Stage Manager's very real artistic responsibilities to a production. SMs are expected to call a show throughout its run. They are also expected to maintain the overall artistic integrity of the production in the director's absence. It is absolutely possible to effectively call a show in a mechanically accurate way, but taking the time to understand the artistic approach and reasoning behind light cues, for example, allows the Stage Manager to play an unseen role in the performance. All of the technical cues begin to breathe with the show, and being able to connect with a production on that level allows the SM to adapt to unexpected changes in a more effective and seamless way.

Being able to engage artistically in a project is also going to support the Stage Manager's ability to maintain a show after opening. Once the designers and director have left, it falls to the Stage Manager to ensure that the artistic quality of the production is maintained throughout the run. Being open to becoming a part of the creative team will help you to support the cast throughout this maintenance process, and to identify what is natural growth and what is counter to the creative team's intention. It will also help you to see small changes in the design and look at the production in a more detailed way, not using a checklist, but, rather, being able to instinctually feel when something is off.

Again, both of these are totally valid ways to see yourself as a Stage Manager. They each suggest a very strong position of the role in the larger process, and just because you see yourself as one of these now does not mean that cannot shift as your career develops. This discussion is very much a personal one and can get a little heady. It mainly is about your personal philosophical approach to the job, and while there may not always be time to dedicate to such introspection, it is worth thinking about from time to time.

Archetypes of Stage Managers

Self-awareness and analysis is a critical skill for any manager. Being charged with overseeing staff, or leading a team, means you need to understand who you are as a leader and how you are perceived by those around you. Through self-reflection you can identify those aspects of your personality that positively impact your professional development, as well as those aspects of others that can be adopted to continue to better yourself. It does not matter how long someone has been working as a stage manager, there is always room to become better. This is a slow process but a constant sense of self-awareness will only help on the journey.

For young Stage Managers, or those who are stepping into a new theatrical discipline, it is natural to emulate the people they are working with. The obvious thought process is that "if this person has this job, they must be good at what they do, and, therefore, are someone to model my own development after." This is unfortunately not always going to be true, and the real trick is to know how to identify what another person does that actually works and only begin absorbing those elements. There are a variety of reasons people get jobs. One of the oldest clichés in the entertainment business is that "it is all about who you know." Clichéd as that statement is, it is true. Nepotism, seniority, and loyalty are all major parts of how the industry works. Sometimes this is a good thing because if you develop a positive enough reputation you will be referred to many employers and will have a fruitful career. In other instances, this may take a negative turn and mean that the best person for the job doesn't actually get hired because someone else is better connected. Don't let this be discouraging though. It should serve as motivation to network. Take advantage of every opportunity you are presented with to meet and work with new people, and be smart about who you choose as your mentors and role models.

As with any field, the longer you work in stage management the more patterns begin to emerge in the kinds of people you work with. Over time, it becomes clear that certain personality traits and interests seem to draw people to the field. Once in the field, Stage Managers tend to pick up the traits of those they work with, leading to a very consistent group of archetypes you will encounter:

Below are the six archetypes that are common among the stage management community. After much conversation with Stage Managers for every discipline, this list has proven to be strongly representative of the field and the majority of Stage Managers will fall into one or more of these archetypes:

1   *The Cranky Curmudgeon*
    This Stage Manager is well seasoned and has been around the block. They have seen it all and are a bit over it all. Rarely are they taken by surprise and often they are set in their ways. Their lack of flexibility can

get in the way of them developing relationships with new companies. They are a great source for stories and advice but can sometimes be difficult to work with, especially when they don't have control over the situation they are working in. After gaining years of experience the same old drama has taken its toll and may have sapped some of their joy.

2 *Everybody's Best Friend*
Often a trait of new Stage Managers, the Jimmy Olsen is eager and frequently anxious to please. Their focus tends to be gaining approval or acceptance on a personal level rather than successfully completing their job. They are frequently steamrolled by their colleagues and lose control of the process. They are ultracompassionate and empathetic, and connect with cast, crew, and designers on a more personal than professional level.

3 *The Workaholic*
This Stage Manager is laser focused and never loses sight of the job at hand. This person tends to be a perfectionist and will do whatever is necessary to successfully complete their task. This level of dedication can come at the expense of interpersonal relationships (personally and professionally) and can prove to create an unapproachable demeanor. Frequently, early career Stage Managers fall into this category in a bid to prove themselves, but this style can become habitual and lead to very capable and efficient but socially isolated Stage Managers.

4 *The Renaissance Person*
This Stage Manager has done, or wants to do, everyone else's jobs. By virtue of their job Stage Managers are participants in all parts of the process and this involvement can lead them to believe they can do it better. They feel like they have a better grasp of directing, lighting, or acting in the show than the people hired to do those things. Often a Stage Manager who understands the work of all departments benefits the show, but one who loses sight of the boundaries of their role can be detrimental.

5 *The Zen Master*
This SM is always calm and always patient. They are rarely thrown or upset and generally go with the flow. They tend to not be overly emotional and try to keep others from getting overly emotional. They approach their leadership role from the point of view of a collaborator

and without an agenda. They often aim to accomplish their goals while allowing others to accomplish theirs, rather than prioritizing one above the other. This person is the epitome of flexibility and simply rolls with the punches.

6 *The Authoritarian*

Whatever their personal motivations this Stage Manager believes that the best way to do their job is to assert absolute control over the process. They tend to micromanage their productions and insist their method is the best. They desire being a one-man-band and can lose track of the needs of others. They will often prioritize their goals over those of the team and lack flexibility. Maintaining a calm demeanor is difficult for them when things do not go according to plan.

It is easy to judge certain of these archetypes as being representative of a good or bad Stage Manager, but the reality is that each has its own positive and negative traits. It is also important to remember that every Stage Manager is going to be a combination of a number of these, and that is how it should be. The goal should be to pull the aspects of these archetypes that are going to be best suited for the type of work you do and compliment your personality.

For example, in the world of industrials and corporate events, a Stage Manager who is a blend of the *Authoritarian, Workaholic*, and *Renaissance Person* is going to be more effective than someone who more closely identifies as *Everybody's Best Friend*. The world of corporate events is fast paced and often requires the Stage Manager to interact with numerous vendors, venue representatives, and larger business entities who do not normally produce theatrical projects. Being someone who is comfortable taking charge and putting the weight of the event on your own shoulders is going to benefit you in that environment. You may find that in these situations you will need to be more direct and hard edged than you might normally prefer. This does not condone unpleasantness, but being a bit harsher is a valid tact to take if the situation requires it. Conversely, if you are working with children, combining *The Zen Master* with a bit of *Everybody's Best Friend* and a dash of *Workaholic* is likely going to get the job done. Leading large casts of children will often require a calm, steady, and dedicated hand in order for the project to be successful.

The role of the Stage Manager is much more than just the tasks they perform. In many ways, the competency and fitness of a Stage Manager is measured more by their ability to work with other people than it is in their skill at creating clean paperwork. The best way to develop and nurture those skills is to spend time looking at how others interact with each other and evaluating how you behave in comparison. Taking the time to evaluate yourself is critical in fine-tuning your ability to work efficiently and effectively in any discipline.

2

Preproduction

Every production, whether a play, musical, concert, special event, etc, begins with a form of preparatory period. These periods can range from years in advance of opening to mere hours before the audience walks into the venue, but every process has to start somewhere. The Stage Manager's role during this period can vary dramatically and, like most things when it comes to stage management, depends on the type of show, who is producing, and your relationship with the company. Generally speaking, the Stage Manager has very little control over what the length of a prep period for a show might be.

In the world of unions, the length of the prep period is determined by the union's contract standards. This time is normally referred to as the "prep week," whether it is a full week or just a couple of days. The "prep week" is a set number of days where the Stage Manager is paid their contracted rate (or some portion of it), with no rehearsal responsibilities. The working hours during the "prep week" are determined by the Stage Manager and, if the theater does not have workspace set aside, they will often even work from home. In nonunion theatre the prep week is often undefined. The Stage Manager is expected to prepare on their own time, often without specific payment for those hours. The remuneration for that work is assumed to be rolled into whatever fee the Stage Manager is receiving. In either situation, the work still needs to get done and it is important for the Stage Manager to feel confident and knowledgeable on the first day of rehearsal. The only way to do that is to take the time to prepare appropriately.

Reading the script

The first step in preparing to work on any show is to take the time to get a sense of what the show actually is. In a perfect world, the Stage Manager should carve out time during their prep period to sit down, read, and break down the script so that they can go into meetings or a first rehearsal with a clear picture of what a show requires. This is, for obvious reasons, a wise choice and will set them up for success from the outset. The reality, however, is that Stage Managers often do not have time to dedicate to doing this outside the rehearsal room, so they will make use of the first read through as their opportunity to dig into the text in a detailed way. This does not mean that they neglect preparing by working to wrap their head around the production itself, but, rather, that they don't dig into the literary side until this moment. Each Stage Manager has their own individual needs and their preparatory style has to service those. No matter when or how the Stage Manager decides to delve into a script, they are all looking for the same details.

Reading a script as a Stage Manager requires a different eye than it does to read it purely for literary understanding, or even as a performer preparing for a role. Stage Managers must read a script with a broad view. While details will become important later, the Stage Manager has to be able to take in the big picture in order to start to piece together the mechanics of a show. While a Scenic Designer may read with a focus on locations and a Costume Designer will put emphasis on articles of clothing that a playwright calls out, the Stage Manager must absorb some amount of everything and parse out what is of importance to their role in the production. While the Stage Manager is not tasked with conceiving the world of the play, they do need to fully understand the mechanics of it prior to stepping into a meeting with a creative team. For example, if they are working on a production of *Miss Saigon* and they walk into a production meeting not knowing that there's a helicopter in the second act, that is going to be a significant issue. It is an issue both in the optics of how the Stage Manager will be perceived by the team, but also that solving this moment should be the first thing on the Stage Manager's mind. A helicopter is obviously a very large and dramatic example of what a Stage Manager is looking for as they read, but there are numerous smaller and more mundane items that the Stage Manager should be flagging as they go, from smoking on stage to fight choreography to stage directions that could create dangerous situations. Flagging these types of details will lead to deeper conversations with the creative team and producers on how to solve them, and, hopefully, make for a smoother and more organized production process.

The initial reading

With time and experience a person can train their eye to pull out the critical details quickly over the course of a single reading, but as you are starting out and honing those skills a broad-view initial reading of the play is a great start. Start by just reading for understanding and not for show-running details. The stage management art form requires that you can think creatively and artistically about a play so that you can engage with and relate to the cast and creative team about their work in a more comprehensive way. If the Stage Manager is looking for just pure mechanics it will be harder for them to be able to anticipate and address the concerns of those around them. In the initial reading of the play, start from a clean slate. Read from the perspective of an audience member who is going to be experiencing it in the theater. Try to identify why the theater has decided to produce this show. Show some respect for the work itself, purely from a literary standpoint. This will also help to get a broader view of the way the show is put together. Having that broad view in your back pocket will make going through and pulling out the details a lot easier. Aiming to gain an understanding of the show artistically also makes the Stage Manager more effective in the discussion of the logistics of why or how something needs to work. Ultimately these conversations come down to the way ideas are framed. An artistic understanding of a piece will allow the Stage Manager to offer alternative suggestions to ideas that may not be possible in a way that is sensitive to the artistic integrity of the show.

The second pass

The second reading of the play should be about understanding various elements. Depending on the complexity of the piece, a second reading may also be the last of the prep period. If the script is very simple and straightforward, with a unit set and minimal props, reading it once for a broad view and then once to understand the mechanics may be enough. If a show is more complex, additional readings may be required to peel back the layers of detail. For example, a show like *Noises Off* will likely require more than two readings. The play (particularly the second act) is almost all stage directions, and the level of detail that is outlined regarding props, costumes, staging, lighting, sound, and stunts is so complicated it is going to be nearly impossible to gain a comprehensive understanding without reading for each area individually.

For a show of this level of complexity the second pass will likely put the focus on scenery and props. These two items are quite naturally linked and it makes sense to combine them when pulling out the details that the script provides. While it is not the responsibility of the Stage Manager to stage a show themselves, reading the play and breaking it apart in a way that anticipates how a director might stage it, allows the Stage Manager to better prepare for needs in the rehearsal room. A stage direction that indicates that a character picks up a glass from the bar on stage right and carries it to the coffee table on stage left, where they then pick up a cigarette and begin smoking, tells the reader a lot of information and will lead the Stage Manager to ask some very important questions, e.g., "Are we using a real glass?", "Is it important to see liquid in the glass?", "Does the cigarette need to be practical?", "Do we need to see a flame when the cigarette is lit?" Flagging these intricate details shows a great degree of engagement and is only going to help to build the sense of respect and trust that the Stage Manager will need to foster with the creative team.

Asking these questions up front will also generate some amount of discussion. It is important for the Stage Manager to know that all the details called out in these questions have some level of concern associated with them. Putting real glass on stage runs the risk of it breaking during the performance and creating a safety hazard for the cast. Having liquid on stage means there is a risk of spilling on costumes or props in addition to the floor and creating a slip hazard. Smoking on stage is a controversial issue, no matter where you go. Some theaters allow it and some do not. Some actors are very sensitive to the idea of smoking or being around smoke, so there are personal concerns to consider. An open flame is always a concern and will need to be approved by the fire marshal at the theater, so if anyone brings up the desire to have flames on stage the Production Manager should be alerted immediately. How the Stage Manager raises these questions is a key building block in developing their relationship with the creative team. It is important to not be alarmist. At the end of the day, at this early stage of the process everything should be able to be discussed. Some things will have clear cut answers; if a theater does not allow smoking on stage then there will be no real smoking, but other questions may require a more nuanced discussion.

If there is not a lot of physical action around the glass items, having them on stage becomes less of a concern. The same is true of liquids. It is important to be a collaborator and not the nay-sayer. Flagging potential issues will show engagement; offering solutions that protect the artistic intention of the production will show investment.

When reading the script with scenery and props in mind, the first and foremost thing to be looking for will be location:

- Where does the play take place?
- How many different locations do you visit over the course of a play?
- Is there any indication of scale noted in the playwright's notes or in stage directions?
- Are there specific references to types of furniture or set dressing and how they are used?

Understanding the scope and scale of what the playwright is asking for is key to getting a full grasp on the show itself. The physical scope of the production says a lot about the style of the show and what the Stage Manager can expect from the production process. Smaller, more intimate shows will likely mean a more personal approach to mounting the production. The Stage Manager can assume that, with a smaller physical scope, more time will be spent in rehearsal forging personal bonds among the cast and sharing ideas about the work. Both of these inferences will directly influence how the Stage Manager might begin to think about the schedule. With a larger show, there will be less time to spend on exploration in the room, so a more organized and heavily planned approach is going to be likely. These are generalities and it is certainly possible for shows that appear intimate on the page to turn into massive physical productions and vice versa, but referencing the physical scope that the playwright has outlined can provide a solid starting point for the Stage Manager to evaluate how to prepare for the coming process.

Once a basic assessment of the scope has been established and a list of the locations for the show has been generated, the Stage Manager can begin digging deeper into the logistical needs of the show:

- Are there references to stairs?
- Do lines of text or stage directions provide insight into where a specific element of the set may be?

If there's a line of dialogue referencing a door to the right of the stairs, that likely means the set will need to include both stairs and a door to the right of them. It is worth noting that stage directions are often pulled from a show's original production's Stage Manager's blocking script. They serve as a way to clarify a reader's experience when reading something that is meant to be seen on stage and are not necessarily requirements when mounting a new production. There are other times, however, when a playwright will provide specific stage directions that are meant to be followed. The requirement to follow the stage directions may be spelled out in the contract for the show or may simply be understood in the theatrical culture. The works of Samuel Beckett are an excellent example of this. Beckett provides a great deal of detail in his stage directions and it is culturally understood that, when mounting one of his plays, you must follow the stage directions to the letter. The entire creative team, as well as the Stage Manager, should be made aware if this type of requirement exists. All of this is to say that, while the immediate temptation may be to skip over stage directions there is quite a bit of useful information to be discovered within them.

There is also substantial value in looking for details about decorative elements on the set and how they are used, which might be pertinent for the Stage Manager to be aware of. Is there an indication that someone leans on banisters, needs to clutch hooks on the wall, or any such thing that might be important to note, so that it can be flagged in a meeting with the creative team to confirm whether this production will do those things or not? These kinds of details inform how things will need to be built or reinforced and can begin a conversation about what it is necessary to have in the rehearsal room. Going back to the example of *Noises Off*, each of the three acts takes place on the set of a play with a staircase and multiple doors. Much of the comedic action has to do with people running up and down those stairs, and opening and closing the doors. Almost the entirety of each act is built around that action. Taking note of the importance of those scenic elements and starting a dialogue about how best to integrate them in the rehearsal process is important. Depending on the resources of the theater that is producing the show, there might be the possibility of rehearsal stairs that could be put in the rehearsal room. Barring that option, some time may need to be included in the schedule once the set is built to either visit the scenic shop and allow the cast to get a feel for what the stairs feel like, or have some dedicated spacing time on stage to translate the room staging to the set. This time would likely need to be much longer than what a normal production might require.

When it comes to props, keeping a notebook nearby and jotting things down as they come up is likely going to be the easiest way to keep track. The

Prop Master will also be doing this, but it's helpful to have a couple of people's eyes on it. The Director will also, hopefully, provide a list of what they feel they require. Being able to take the notes of multiple people and compare them to create the final list will lead to a more comprehensive and accurate list. Depending on the show and the level at which it is being produced, the Stage Manager may not get too heavily involved in the conversation about the prop list until one exists, but having some frame of reference from the script will help to understand the scope of the show.

Remember that there's overlap between scenery and props, and taking note of couches, settees, dining room tables, and specifics on chairs is wise; while the Scenic Designers may be the ones that have final say on them, the Prop Master may be the one sourcing those items. Knowing how the furniture is to be utilized will help to flag any adjustments that need to be made to the items. Often the Prop Master will ask all of those questions of the Director, but if the show does not have a dedicated Prop Master it will fall to the Stage Manager to track those details and communicate what needs to be done. If people are just sitting at the dining room table there is nothing to flag, but if someone climbs on top of the chair, or the table itself, whoever is providing the items will need to know that. Think through whether the action that is required will dictate the kind of item sourced and any special modifications that might need to be made to it.

The third pass

Reading the script with an eye towards lighting and costume would be the third pass on the script. Most scripts do not specifically call out a lot of detail regarding lighting. They often speak more in terms of mood and atmosphere than very specific cues, so it makes sense to pair that department with one that will likely have much more detail called out in the script. Similar to scenery, wardrobe items don't need the Stage Manager to identify everything just the elements that will impact the cast in a very specific way. The Costume Designer will, obviously, determine how the script will inform the final design of the clothing, but the Stage Manager can help in that process by flagging how the clothing will interact with the action on stage. For example, pockets are something that tend to get overlooked quite frequently, so it can be very helpful for the Stage Manager to consider how costumes will work in conjunction with props as they read. If the script indicates that a character is supposed to pull a flask out of their jacket pocket, flagging that early will help to ensure a conversation about whether the Director intends to stage that moment into the show, whether the Costume Designer has accounted for a flask-size pocket, and whether the Prop Master needs to prioritize finding the right flask so that the pocket can be built. The need for additional pockets will almost certainly arise during the course of rehearsals. It's one of the most common things that comes up, but also one of the most frequently forgotten things in the preparation period. The earlier these discussions occur the less stress there will be on the Stage Manager later to communicate those things, and the higher likelihood that they will get done.

The last department, which can fit into any pass that makes sense for the show, is sound. Due to wide variance in the way sound is used in shows, it is hard to pigeonhole or directly connect it to any other discipline. For some shows, the sound design is more important than the scenery and other shows do not have any sound beyond the acoustic sound of the actors voices. After getting through the first pass it should be clear how critical sound is to the particular show you are analyzing, and that will make the determination of when and how you focus on it. It is important to look at how integrated the sound design is to the production, and often this is something that cannot be gleaned from reading the script. Unless the playwright has been very specific, there is invariably going to need to be a conversation with the Director and Designer to determine how important it would be to have sound playback in the rehearsal room, for example.

Reading with this level of detail will not only better the preparedness of the SM, but also help to elevate them in the eyes of their peers. Having this information at their fingertips will help the Stage Manager to better anticipate the needs of the creative team and cast, and will make for a smoother process overall. Again, it is often hard to find the time to dedicate to this level of detailed analysis but, over time, the skills to pull out the important information and bypass the less critical will develop, making this kind of analysis a little easier to accomplish and finding the time to do it more realistic.

The prep week

Almost every professional contract is going to outline some kind of preparation period for the Stage Manager to put together all of their materials prior to the start of rehearsals. These prep periods can be as short as a day or two, or as long as a couple of weeks, depending on the size and scale of the show and the financial resources of the company. The start of the prep period also coincides with the moment that the Stage Manager(s) become "on contract." This means that they are now officially being paid by the production for their time. One of the interesting understandings that exists around the prep period is that, while it may be outlined as a certain number of days or hours within the week leading up to the start of rehearsals, that time can be reallocated and used in advance of the official week if the Stage Manager is willing. Right from the moment of hiring, the Stage Manager may be asked to attend meetings, participate in emailing, generate schedules, or any number of time consuming tasks before officially starting to receive checks from the producers. Professionally, these types of duties are outlined and presented up front. Different companies organize this workload in different ways. Usually the number of production meetings or additional duties that the Stage Manager is expected to participate in is outlined in the contract at the time of hiring. Things always change, so flexibility is key, but understanding the expectations of the company you will be working with in the preproduction timeframe is important.

One of the largest sticking points when it comes to these ancillary meetings and extra bits of work is the idea of exclusivity. Exclusivity refers to the idea that the Stage Manager cannot work on another project during the same timeframe. Once on contract, the Stage Manager is generally assumed to be exclusive to a single show. In practice, it is not uncommon for Stage Managers to take multiple gigs simultaneously, but it is their own responsibility to ensure that the multiple jobs do not hinder each other. The Stage Manager's participation in any activities related to the show prior to their official start date are completely optional, unless otherwise negotiated at the time of contracting. Sometimes it is going to be incredibly helpful to participate, but there is no obligation. If the Stage Manager is engaged on another project when some of these ancillary activities come up, it is important to obtain clearance from the producer who is currently paying them before committing to doing things for the other show. At the end of the day, whoever is paying you currently must take precedence over the person who is paying you in the future. This means that sometimes saying no to attending a production meeting is going to be necessary. New Stage Managers are often taken advantage of because they struggle to draw that boundary line, but know that it is ok to say no. An individual's obligation to a show does not kick in until their formal start date.

Production meetings

Each show has many different people, all collaborating to get something on the stage for the audience to see. The key to that collaborative process is, obviously, to talk to each other, but that becomes difficult when designers and other creative team members are spread across multiple states or countries, or are otherwise unavailable to sit around a table and discuss. Throughout the preproduction process, long before the Stage Manager gets involved, there are many email, phone, or Skype meetings that occur, but rarely does everyone get to sit in the same room. With the ease of email, it has also become progressively rarer to get a full team on the phone together. Design meetings tend to include only the required parties for a specific topic, which means things can fall through the cracks when the folks on the call don't think through, or don't realize, how their choices are impacting other departments.

Once the ball is rolling, and there's a semiclear view of how a show is moving forward, putting together a group meeting that incorporates the production team and the entire design team sitting around a table together is critical. Most frequently these production meetings are assembled by the Producer or Production Manager. Due to the inherent difficulty in scheduling them, there tend to only be only a couple of production meetings on most shows. The expectation is that individual team members and departments are talking outside of these meetings, so when everyone does get together it is important to try bring everyone up to speed on the progress of the show and to focus on those details that require input from the larger team. Also, thanks to technology, more and more of these meetings are being done over the phone (either conference or video calling). The structure of these meetings varies from show to show and company to company. Depending on where you're working, the main Producer or Production Manager may run the meeting. It is also very possible that the Stage Manager will be asked to take the lead.

Tips and tricks for running a production meeting

Welcome and introduction

It is customary to go around the table and have everyone introduce themselves and their roles on the production. Even if many people around the table or on the phone have worked together before, it is always nice to provide the reminder and ensure everyone has been introduced. Less common, but a nice touch, is to set out name cards visible to the rest of the people at the table to help everyone learn each other's names. Sometimes this can feel a little formal, but when there are tons of new people in the room it can be a very useful tool. However you choose to do these introductions, the most important thing is to make sure that a welcoming atmosphere is established for everyone. It is important for the Stage Manager to help set that tone. No matter how stressful a show may be, or how high tensions may have become outside the meeting room, everyone needs to come to the table with an open mind, ready to collaborate.

Meeting structure

As with so many things in the world of stage management, the way a meeting is structured depends on the situation. Depending on the stage in the process that the meeting takes place in, you may focus on broad strokes or be able to get into the nitty gritty detail. No matter what, the Stage Manager should come into the meeting with an agenda. Have something mapped out and distribute it to everyone in the room, so that everyone is working from the same page. One of the most frustrating elements of production meetings is that they tend to wander. Everyone in the room has their own priorities that they want to address and will try to steer the conversation towards those topics. Though a topic may feel imperative to an individual, it may not be the most pressing action item. By listing the topics for discussion out on paper, people will see that their issue is allotted a time to be addressed and they're less likely to try and jump over everyone else to get to it. In order to get a list of what everyone wants to talk about, the Stage Manager needs to reach out to them well in advance of the meeting. Sending out individual emails to the creative team and any other attendees, asking them to provide topics of interest can be very helpful in generating an agenda for the meeting and making sure that it is comprehensive. Contacting them individually is not simply a suggestion. Doing this will ensure that you have direct contact with them. It provides the Stage Manager with the chance to introduce themselves and begin a dialogue with each of the collaborators they will be working with. An unpersonalized mass email is less likely to get a response and does not get your relationship off to a great start.

Who goes first

Despite the fairly casual and collaborative environment that is the theatre, production meetings tend to bring out the ego in everybody. Depending on who you're working with, people can be very sensitive about whose issue is addressed first. Generally speaking, a meeting will begin with a welcome from the Stage Manager or whoever is leading the meeting, and then go to the Director for any general updates and thoughts. It is important to try to contain these initial remarks from the Director to general updates and not let them deviate to topics that are already laid out on the agenda. This is the first moment that the meeting will have the chance to start to wander, so it needs to be carefully managed. One of the best ways to manage that is to have a sidebar with the Director prior to the meeting. Have a chat about what the plans are for the meeting, in the same way that you are reaching out to everyone else about the topics they want to address. Make sure the Director is onboard with how the meeting will be organized and they will then be able to help keep things on track, or at least support the person who is. Following the initial Director's remarks, the structure for the remainder of the meeting will come down to the priority list that the Stage Manager, or meeting leader, has compiled in the agenda. In most cases these meeting are organized by department rather than issue, but there is flexibility in that, of course. The standard is to go department by department to discuss the pertinent issues involving each. If the production meeting is happening at a stage when the show is still loose and conceptual, it may be more useful to have the Director talk about the concept and then allow the designers to ask questions to start a dialogue. This approach also generates a brainstorming session for everyone to solve the show as a group. Be thoughtful in the way that you organize a meeting. Understand that there is limited time and so it must be used wisely.

Managing the conversation

As previously stated, production meetings tend to go off on tangents and it falls to the Stage Manager, or whoever is leading the meeting, to try and bring people back to the topic at hand. People will get passionate about one thing or another and will tend to want to focus there, but the meeting leader needs to be able to filter that passion and try to serve everyone at the table. Keeping an eye on the clock and having an awareness of how people in the room are holding up are the two keys to doing this well. Over time it becomes easier to decipher people's body language and figure out who is frustrated, antsy, bored, etc. That information is all useful as you pace out the meeting and allow certain conversations to go on longer than others. Sometimes a topic will arise that needs to be talked out in that moment, even if it does not involve everyone at the table. It is okay to allow that to happen, but the Stage Manager needs to be discerning and understand which conversations are so imperative they should waste other people's time, and which aren't. For example, it can be very useful for the Lighting Designer to listen to conversation about set dressing in the event a lamp or other light source is added. It is less useful for the Lighting Designer to listen to a conversation about the texture of a throw on the sofa. Figuring out which is appropriate for a production meeting and which isn't is a skill learned over time, but one that needs to be developed in order to be successful.

The Stage Manager's kit

Being a Stage Manager is a little bit like being a scout. There's an expectation of the person in that position to always be prepared for any eventuality that might arise. Part of this is intellectually being able to process and problem-solve on the fly and the other is a level of physical preparedness for anything that may come up during the course of rehearsals and performances. This means that the Stage Manager needs to be fully supplied with anything that could be useful at any moment. This stockpile of supplies is generally referred to as a Stage Manager's "kit." The items found in the kit are wide and varied, and there are no hard and fast rules that govern what goes in there. Some SMs prefer to travel light, while others bring everything but the kitchen sink. Both are valid ways to work and the appropriateness of each comes down to the work situation.

There are certain fundamental elements that a Stage Manager is going to need, and they are rooted in common sense. Basic office supplies, medical supplies, pens and notebooks, Band-Aids, painkillers, paperclips, tape, stapler, ruler, and scissors are all going to be useful. The real question is where to go from there? The best way to assemble your kit is to start with the things you personally need to do the job. Get your favorite office supplies. If there is a particular type, size, or color of sticky note you prefer, stock that. From there look to your own experience. During a past rehearsal were you ever asked for something that you did not have handy? Perhaps that should be added to the kit. Certain types of shows also will generate ideas of what to have available. Shows with dance might inspire the Stage Manager to keep a supply of ace bandages and ice packs handy. If there is ballet, having a small package of rosin might not be a bad idea. Shows with singing might prompt you to have various teas or similar in the kit. Whatever items might come to mind, always remember that although the Stage Manager is not responsible for supplying these items, there is an expectation that the Stage Manager will have some basic essentials on hand.

Stage management kits are furnished by the Stage Manager and, depending on the organization that you're working with, you may or may not receive some level of reimbursement for the supplies that you're putting into it. Generally speaking, as a freelance Stage Manager there is a certain belief that the basics of a SM kit are to be supplied by the freelancer, because that is what is required for them to do their job. This is almost equated to a chef who brings their own knives or an electrician who has their own wrench. Theaters with less resources tend to expect that the Stage Manager will provide their own kit, free of charge. In certain circumstances, Stage Managers will charge a kit rental fee. This is a completely reasonable thing to do. There is no reason why your paycheck should be going to furnish the kit when it is the cast and crew that is depleting it. Just know that this is not the wide-sweeping standard, and so you may or may not receive some level of pushback.

Many long-standing companies will have their own stage manager kits. These are furnished by the company, and over the years many Stage Managers will have contributed suggestions of what should be added. These kits are always a wonderful resource, as the Stage Manager is not burdened with the responsibility of replenishing their own kits. The more often they can save their supplies for the moments when they are really needed, the better. It also removes some of the financial burden without needing to negotiate a rental fee in their contract. That being said, most SMs take a lot of pride in their kits and will put time and creativity into developing something that they can showcase as being uniquely their own. For young Stage Managers especially, having just the right thing when asked becomes a game or challenge. Embracing this kind of challenge is what leads to finding some very odd elements in people's kits, but those odd items often tell the story of an individual's career. These items can be as simple as safety pins and miniature sewing kits (which are a relatively standard item to find in a Stage Manager's kit) or underwear, food coloring—even extra yoga mats. Some Stage Managers travel with whole number lines in their kits. These are usually long, thin stretches of fabric that already have dance numbers painted onto them. These can be incredibly useful when you find that you need numbers for spacing performers and you can just roll this out. It is an odd item to have, but it makes the SM look incredibly prepared and can often make the SM stand out in the Director or Choreographer's mind in the future. There are some who travel with basic prop items. These might include a couple of glasses, an ashtray, or articles of clothing, so they're ready for the moment the Director wants to add a hat or scarf to the scene. If you find yourself working outdoors, bug spray and sunscreen are great items to have in your kit, both for yourself and to help out the cast.

Each person is unique in what they feel is necessary to have with them in their kits, but it's also completely possible to go overboard. The level of appropriateness of the kit can usually be judged by the case that holds the items. Small toolboxes and duffel bags are common choices. Diaper bags are a great option, as they already have built-in pockets of various sizes. Rolling suitcases are also popular to allow the Stage Manager to carry a lot of material without having to physically carry a heavy bag. Some Stage Managers have been known to bring their kit in large, waist-height, rolling tool cabinets. These might be overkill for a show where the company is providing a kit, but in certain circumstances could be completely appropriate. If the container makes sense for the transport of the items you are bringing and your physical ability to easily move it around, it is the right choice.

Preparing the prompt book

The single most important item that the Stage Manager produces over the course of a production is the prompt book. The prompt book is the Stage Manager's archive of all information about a production. It is how the Stage Manager organizes themselves from the beginning of the preproduction process through to the last performance. It is also what is turned over to the producers at the conclusion of a contract to be held for future productions. While the majority of the information and documentation that goes into a prompt book is generated during the rehearsal process, the book needs to be prepared during preproduction.

The form that the book takes has started to change in recent years. Traditionally it was a large, tabbed binder that contained hard copies of every piece of paperwork associated with a show. Many companies still insist on the hard copy version as a safety net, however, more and more are moving to a fully digital archive. Many Stage Managers also prefer to work in a more paperless way. This cuts down on the level of bulk and heft that they are carrying around throughout the process, and is more environmentally friendly. The reality is that documents related to a show are always being updated and changed, and so, in order to keep the book up to date, you are constantly printing version after version of the same piece of paper. Staying paperless makes for a more eco-friendly way to approach the process. There are drawbacks, however. It is usually much faster and easier to pull up a hard copy of a document you need, than to have numerous folders open on the computer and wait for a document to load. Computers have a finite battery, and if the Stage Manager is working in an environment where wall outlets are limited they can find their hands tied. Many people who go the paperless route also like to use online file-storage services, such as Dropbox or GoogleDocs. While incredibly useful services, if you are without an internet connection you may not be able to access a file you really need. Whichever route is chosen, hard copy or digital, the Stage Manager should make that decision during preproduction. Getting the basic structure of the book set up in advance is going to help tremendously in the long run.

The sections of the book

- *Table of Contents*: This is most pertinent in a hard copy version. Usually the table of contents will only list the general sections of the book and not the individual documents themselves. In the case of a digital version, the table of contents will just be the names of the file folders in your master "Prop Book" folder.
- *Contact Sheet*: The Stage Manager will generate a contact sheet for the creative team and cast. Both should be kept confidential unless the parties included say it can be distributed. This is one of the most important items in the SMs arsenal so having a hard copy is important.
- *Blocking Script*: The blocking script is a full printout of the script, which includes notation that outlines all performer movement in a given production.
- *Calling/Prompt Script*: This copy of the script contains all technical cues and is what the Stage Manager will use to call the show. Sometimes the calling and blocking scripts are combined to be on the same printout,

and sometimes the Stage Manager will have two separate copies of the script.

- *Scenery*: This serves as a living archive of documentation related to the scenery for a show. Ground plans, section drawings, photos, and any other pertinent items that have been received from the Designer or scenic shop should be filed here for future reference and use. Running paperwork related to the set that is generated by the SM team will also be included here as it develops throughout the process.
- *Props*: This section will include prop lists, prop photos, drawings, and any other documentation related to props. In the final archive this will also include the detailed props running paperwork that stage management will create.
- *Costumes*: Aside from the archiving purposes, it can be very useful to have copies of the Costume Designer's renderings handy in rehearsals. Questions about what someone is wearing in a given scene come up regularly and having a photo reference can be very helpful. Any costume inventories or running documentation is also going to go here.
- *Hair and Makeup*: This section may sometimes be combined with costumes, depending on the complexity of the design. This section is almost solely for the final archiving of the production. Unless the show has a very intricate hair design that would impact actor movement, it is rare to include much more than a run sheet until the final archiving of the book.
- *Lighting*: Like the hair and makeup section, the lighting section is mostly going to be about the final archive. It is rare to even have lighting paperwork when the rehearsal process starts. Once you receive it, including the plot can be helpful, and obviously the cue sheet is a necessity for the final archiving.
- *Sound*: Again, most shows do not have physical sound paperwork ready before tech, but getting a hold of a cue sheet to have as a reference as early as you can is very wise.
- *Rehearsal Reports*: All rehearsal reports should be archived in the final version of the prompt book. Some people print them and add them to the book on a daily basis, but this will add a lot of heft to your book over time so it can be easier to hold off on printing until the end.

Ultimately, the preproduction process is about the Stage Manager's personal comfort more than anything else. While much of the work that they do will make everything run smoother for the rest of the people involved in a show, the few days they have to work on their own is about making sure they feel ready for the coming weeks of active production. It is the one opportunity to take their time to really ensure that they feel confident stepping into rehearsal on the first day. While there are certain things that are expected of the Stage Manager during this time, there are no hard and fast rules about how they get it done. It is also the moment the Stage Manager has to start to build the foundation of their relationship with their team of ASMs. Sometimes they are included in preproduction and sometimes they are not, but the Stage Manager should still be reaching out to them to make sure they feel like they are a welcome part of the process. Using the time that is allotted to make sure you feel ready is the key to a successful rehearsal process, because from this moment on things start to get really busy.

3

The Production Process: Room Rehearsal

The first day of rehearsal is the culmination of months, perhaps years, of preparation on the Director's part, and weeks of work getting up to speed for the Stage Manager. The term "rehearsal" refers to the work sessions that allow the cast to develop their performances and physically put a show together. Over the course of the rehearsal period, however long it may be, the cast is staged into the show and learn what they're going to be doing when it comes time for the audience. The rehearsal period is also the time when the cast, creative team, and Stage Managers come together and develop the dynamic that will carry them through the entire run of the show. This is the moment that the stage management team has the opportunity to build a strong foundation of trust with both the cast and Director.

Rehearsals are usually conducted in an alternate space prior to moving to the stage. It is very rare for a show to get to rehearse on stage from the first day, because it's generally far too expensive to gain access and operate a theater for more than a limited number of technical rehearsals and performances. The fact that everyone working on a given show is normally isolated in an off-site rehearsal room also encourages the building of a strong bond, which will be incredibly important throughout all aspects of the show-mounting process.

Every rehearsal process is going to be different and that is a part of the fun of walking in on the first day. With all the time and effort that is put into preparing for that moment, there is really no way to truly know what the room will be like once all of the varied personalities are in the same place at the same time. This is also the moment the Stage Manager gets to step into the fire and start problem-solving on the fly. There will always be unforeseen hiccups and hurdles to be jumped and this is the moment where all of that really begins. It can feel like, and is often referred to as, the first day of school. No matter how many first days of rehearsal one has been through, there is always the same sense of anxiety and anticipation that can only be compared to being a kid and walking into school on the first day of a new year.

"Running rehearsals"

The central, and most visible job of the Stage Manager during the rehearsal process is to "run" the rehearsals. This means that they oversee all aspects of how a rehearsal is organized and strive to support accomplishing the Director's goals for the rehearsal each day. This support includes working to maintain a highly efficient and well-ordered nature to the logistics of each rehearsal. While the Stage Manager cannot dictate the way in which a Director or Choreographer utilizes their time, nor the pace at which a cast member works, they can make sure that no ancillary issues slow the process. Their role can often feel like clearing the path for the creative team to be able to work. By thinking ahead and asking questions they are able to hopefully clear potential distractions and obstacles in order to avoid delays to the process.

One of the most useful services a Stage Manager can provide in the rehearsal room is serving as an objective set of eyes on the process. Often, the cast and creative team can become too close to the work and cannot see the forest for the trees. Periodically there will be roadblocks and it becomes hard to see potential solutions to time and logistical problems in the moment. This is not a negative reflection on them and, in fact, simply represents how deeply invested in the work they are. The Stage Manager's role in running rehearsals is to look at the big picture and think ahead to what is required to keep things moving and on track. As you try to accomplish this goal don't be afraid to voice suggestions that might be able to save time and maintain efficiency. The offering of these suggestions needs to be tempered by reading the room and identifying the appropriateness of such intervention, but it is more frequently met with openness and gratitude rather than opposition. The Stage Manager should feel like an active participant in the process, and the more actively they engage in what is happening the easier it will become to drive the rehearsals in a more efficient direction. As another collaborator in the room, the Stage Manager will find that they become more empowered to do their job with a certain autonomy, and the trust of their colleagues will begin to build.

As a part of the endeavor to provide structure to the rehearsal process, one of the SM's major responsibilities will lie in the realm of scheduling. In conjunction with the Director's needs for a given rehearsal, the Stage Manager will set the calls for the actors to ensure they are present, call breaks, provide administrative support within the room, and logistically make the rehearsals run smoothly. There is a risk and a history of Stage Managers being viewed as administrative assistants due to these duties, but it is important to remember that these are only a fraction of the functions of the Stage Manager in the larger process. Directors and cast members, particularly old-school ones, can sometimes view stage management as support staff, rather than collaborators. This is an unfortunate reality of theatrical culture and while that perception has started to dissipate, there is still a ways to go and it will only be changed over time. One of the best ways to combat this antiquated perception is for the Stage Manager to actively engage in the process. A passive posture, one that only responds to the needs of the room and is never proactive, will only support the notion that the stage management team is separate from everyone else, rather than their teammates.

All of this being said, the administrative functions of the Stage Manager are critical to the success of every production. While some may view breaks as a nuisance that disrupt the flow of a rehearsal, ensuring that everyone in the room has an opportunity to step away from the work for a few moments at times is quite important. People need a moment to reset, and while there are certainly times where the momentum of the rehearsal is interrupted it does not negate the necessity.

They become even more critical when working in a union situation. Almost universally the theatre industry's standard break schedule is based on the Actor's Equity Association (AEA) contract standard. The AEA requires a five-minute break every fifty-five minutes, or a ten-minute break every eighty minutes. In the opera world the American Guild of Musical Artists (AGMA) sets their own break rules. These are significantly different than the rules in theatre, but in the opera world—union or not—what is established by AGMA sets the standard. The opera standard is a three-hour rehearsal with thirty minutes of break contained within. The opera structure is much more flexible than a professional theatre's structure, with the only requirement being that there be a mandatory break after ninety minutes. If working in a nonunion setting, these are general guidelines more than hard-and-fast rules, but if working in a union setting these need to be followed very strictly as the production could get into significant trouble with the union if they aren't.

One of the areas of real sensitivity for the Stage Manager is negotiating how to call breaks without having a negative effect on the rehearsal that is in progress. Sometimes the Director or actors will be in the zone and not ready to break but the clock is coming up on a mandatory stopping point. The best way to help the Director to manage their time to avoid getting into an awkward situation where you have to bring the rehearsal to a grinding halt, is to provide updates on time when you can. This means if there's a lull in the rehearsal, letting the Director know how much time is remaining before the next break can help them to pace their progress. Sometimes a lull isn't necessary and you can quickly catch their eye to communicate that information. Have a conversation with the Director at the beginning of the rehearsal process and find out exactly how they want this information communicated. Some people prefer a five-minute warning, some prefer a ten, and some would rather not think about it and will give the Stage Manager carte blanche to interrupt as needed. Establishing a system for communicating about time from the beginning will set you up for success in handling breaks. There is a certain nuanced balance to the way that the Stage Manager helps to pace out rehearsals so that breaks flow naturally. It is an unspoken skill that becomes second nature over time. Being able to maintain this fluidity also helps to foster a more positive relationship with the creative team, as they will not feel hindered by the breaks but, rather, ready for them.

Preparing the space

Even before rehearsals begin, one of the first duties of the stage management team is going to be laying out the rehearsal room. The most critical element of preparing the rehearsal room for the arrival of the cast and creative team is "taping out the set." This phrase refers to drawing out the ground plan of the stage and set design on the floor of the rehearsal room using colored tape. The goal is to provide everyone in the rehearsal room with a full-size picture of what they're going to be working with on stage. It's rare to have actual scenery in the rehearsal room, so often all the cast will have to get a sense of spacing is the tape. Providing an accurately sized playing space is obviously critical. This process forces the Stage Manager to process the set design in a very detailed way. Often, just glancing at a ground plan is not going to be enough to fully understand the implications of how the set and staging will interact. However, when put in the position of having to break down the set into inches and feet, the stage management team develops an intensely detailed relationship with the set design.

The first step to correctly taping out the rehearsal space is acquiring a scaled ground plan of the set and stage. A ground plan is a blueprint of the set as seen from above. It will provide the true measurements for all aspects of the set and where things exist in relation to the physical architecture of the theater. The ground plan is generated by the Scenic Designer and will come to the Stage Manager from them directly or by way of the producer. An architect's scale rule is going to be necessary to be able to pull accurate measurements from the drawing, unless someone has the appropriate CAD (computer-aided design) program necessary to pull the dimensions off the drawing. There are a number of different scales that are used in scenic drafting, and the one that is selected usually has to do with being able to fit the set, or theater, onto a reasonably sized piece of paper. Most ground plans are delivered in ¼ inch = 1 foot or ½ inch = 1 foot scale. The scale for a drawing can usually be found in a box on the right-hand side of the drawing. Take the time to double-check the scaling, and if it is not labeled ask the Designer. There is nothing worse than trying to tape out a set in the wrong scale. It is also critical to make sure that measurements are being pulled from the correct side of the scale rule to avoid this same mistake.

Below are some tips on the best method to tape out a floor. Stage Managers develop the system that works best for them, so experiment and see what makes sense. Taping is a combination of math and a connect-the-dots puzzle, so a lot of trial and error will be required before landing on what works for each person.

Tips to tape-out the floor

1. Start with the centerline

The center of the stage is usually represented on the ground plan with a dotted and dashed line that runs vertically from the top of the drawing to the bottom. If for whatever reason it is not there, measure the width of the proscenium (or visible edges of the playing space) to find the center and then draw that line straight through. Be careful not to measure the center off the extreme edges of the theater's architecture, as one side of the backstage area is often larger than the other, which will throw off the center mark. Repeat this process in the rehearsal room. Identify where you plan to place the active playing space for rehearsals. This may mean starting the portion of the stage that audiences will see a few feet away from the actual walls of the room. Lay down a line (which will serve as the downstage edge of the playing space) of the correct width, and mark the center of that with a large "T." Next, lay down the tape measure with "0" on the center mark and the rest going straight upstage. Tape it securely in place.

2. Make the dots

From here, start taking measurements in the divided space created by the centerline. Identify the first corner of each piece of scenery and measure upstage along the centerline. Once the upstage dimension is measured, measure from the centerline straight over to the corner you want to start with. Once these dimensions have been obtained, repeat the procedure full scale on the floor of the rehearsal room and put down a dot of spike tape. Continue in this way until all the points have been laid for that piece of scenery.

3. Connect the dots

Now that the measuring and math is over, it's time for the fun portion: play connect-the-dots. It is entirely a personal preference whether this is done once all the points of the set are down on the ground or if it is done as each connection dot is completed. Either method is totally viable, and depending on the set it may be better to do it one way or the other. It is critical to go back and look at the drawing with each line drawn. Make sure that the two correspond rather than waiting until the end to check, as errors will almost certainly occur along the way. It will be much easier to correct those in the moment, rather than having to pull and retape sections just when it seems to be done.

4. Have a helper

Unless there is no other choice, do not tape the space alone. It's going to take infinitely longer alone and it can be a great bonding exercise for a new stage management team. Just from a practical standpoint, trying to lay a 44-foot-long straight line by yourself is going to be complicated. It can be done, but it's likely going to be a very frustrating experience. Taping the floor, and stage management in general, is a difficult enough job, so make it easier whenever possible.

5. Additional tips

One of the big challenges of taping out the rehearsal room is keeping the tape lines looking clean. From the outset of taping, the goal is to create a rehearsal taping that looks as crisp as the ground plan that is being replicated. There are three main challenges to creating that clean look:

I Straight lines:

Despite measuring carefully, if you start slightly off in one place all of a sudden the whole taping can look cock-eyed. One of the key ways to avoid a crooked rehearsal room is to use the architecture of the space to your advantage when taping straight lines. If there is a wood floor, use the seams of the floor. If the floor itself doesn't provide guidelines to follow, sometimes estimating what looks parallel to the wall can give the appearance of straightness. Use the resources available and don't be afraid to sacrifice absolute dimensional accuracy for visual accuracy. This is not to suggest that skewing dimensions is an acceptable approach, but if the difference of an inch provides a straighter appearance to the eye it can be worthwhile to give up the accuracy. It can often be more jarring, for all parties, to work in a space that looks wrong than a space that is actually slightly wrong. Little variations are not going to impact the cast and Director's ability to stage a production as dramatically as feeling off-kilter the entire time will.

II Corners:

Next to straight lines the most common frustration when taping is getting 90-degree corners. Even if the two lines that are intersecting look straight when they come together they somehow wind up acute or obtuse. This tends to happen without a clear reason and will drive the Stage Managers crazy. When taping a 90-degree angle use a credit card, or any other square edge, to help get the angle to look just right. As with straight lines, visual accuracy can make all the difference to the way people feel while they work in the room.

III Circles and arcs:

Circles are the bane of almost every Stage Manager's professional existence. Taking a straight piece of tape and trying to make it into a smooth curve is, in short, a challenge. It usually means having to go back to geometry class to make these work. First, identify the center point of the circle on the ground plan and translate that to the rehearsal room floor. Now measure the radius of the circle or arc and lay down a reference mark on the floor, from the center point that has already been identified. From here there are a couple of options. The tape measure can be used as a compass to lay down a number of reference marks so that there are dots to connect. This method makes a lot of sense as it allows one more time, unencumbered, to make sure all of the measurements are correct. The other option also involves using the tape measure as a compass, only this time rather than putting dots the tape is used to actually draw the circle as you go. While this can be a more cumbersome way to draw a circle, it does help to give a cleaner round as the tape guides the curve and an individual is not trying to form the curve as they connect the dots. It takes practice to become good at taping curves but every Stage Manager should be ready to take the challenge. There is always a great sense of accomplishment on the other side and it is a frustrating experience that bonds the whole SM community. Be prepared for the first attempts to look terrible and embrace the fact that it will take a few tries to create something that you feel comfortable with.

Once everything is taped and looks beautiful, the team has to emotionally prepare for the reality that it will get messed up almost immediately. As soon as people start walking on it and furniture gets moved around, the tape will get dirty and the lines broken. Maintaining the tape is important, but be reasonable about how frequently it is done. Try not to feel pressured to constantly fix every rip in the tape. Perhaps set aside a moment at the beginning of every week to fix the most significantly damaged areas. The reality is that it will never look as good as it did on the first day, and it is a functional piece of the process, not art that needs to be protected and preserved.

Rehearsal room layout

The rehearsal room is broken up into a few zones of activity. The first is the primary staging space. This is where the set is taped out and all of the actual rehearsing will take place. The next is the production tables. This is the area where the creative team and Stage Manager will sit during the course of the rehearsals. Usually the tables are oriented to replicate the audience perspective. If the rehearsal room has mirrors, it is important to discuss with the Director and Choreographer, if applicable, how they would like to orient the room in relation to the mirrors before you tape out. Depending on the type of show, mirrors can be an asset or a significant distraction. Once this is established, identify how many people will be attending rehearsals on a daily basis. It can safely be assumed that space will be needed for the Director, the Stage Manager, Assistant Stage Managers, and Assistant Director. It's also helpful to have one spare chair for a producer or designer to pop in and watch rehearsals.

Usually the Director and stage management team have separate workspaces in the rehearsal room. One table will be dedicated to the Director and their assistant, and one table for stage management. Stage management also, of course, has satellite stations around the room since the ASMs are going to need to be mobile. In addition to the tables, it's always a nice idea to create a viewing gallery in the room. This is an area of chairs set off to the side so that the cast can sit and watch the rehearsal as they wait.

The final zone of the rehearsal room is the "backstage" area. This will consist of space for prop tables, costume racks, furniture storage, and other elements that will be used sporadically during the rehearsals. All of these items should be organized so that the cast is able to grab what they need and stage management is able to begin to organize how things will be on stage. For example, prop tables are often situated near the entry points to the set, as they will be in real life. In addition to replicating the spacing on stage, trying to create a sense of what the backstage flow is going to be will be very helpful in creating an effective rehearsal process. Creating a simulated version of the backstage area in the rehearsal room will allow the Stage Managers and cast to suss-out potential issues, bottlenecks, and how things need to be laid out when the move to the stage occurs. Stage management should take advantage of the rehearsal process to start to build what they need for the actual running of the show backstage. Room rehearsals are there for Stage Managers as much as for the Director and the cast, so make the most out of them. A greater sense of preparation in the rehearsal room will translate to a much smoother run of the show on stage.

Blocking notation

Possibly the most critical responsibility of the Stage Manager during the rehearsal process is to accurately record the staging of all cast members as it is established. This is important for a number of reasons. The first, and most obvious, is to ensure that everyone remembers what has been set. The second is to provide a reference for the entire creative team during the initial mounting of the production and for any future remounting of the show. This is done through what's called "blocking" notation. "Blocking" is any movement on the stage that does not fall into the classification of choreography. This means each time an actor walks around, picks up a glass, or jumps on a couch is considered blocking and should be carefully recorded. Dance and fight choreography are a bit of a gray area. Usually the Choreographer associated with either discipline will have their own method of recording the movements. The movements also tend to stray into more technical terminology than the Stage Manager may have knowledge of. If a member of the team is well versed in the terms, and even if they are not, they should feel free to create their own record, it will just not serve as the final and lasting record of the show.

There are a variety of ways that a director will choose to block shows, and the method of taking notation will need to adapt to whatever style the Director has adopted. A common rehearsal style is one that is very specifically thought out in advance. The Director knows precisely where people need to go at what moment. Directors who approach staging in this way likely have their own notes in their script. It becomes very easy for the Stage Manager to record this blocking because the record already exists. When Directors prestage a show with this level of detail there is usual minimal deviation from it, at least initially, so the Stage Manager will have ample opportunity to record it themselves and not have to keep up with constant changes. They may even be able to borrow the Director's script and copy over the Director's notes, but that is less common.

Most contemporary theatre employs an "organic" blocking style. "Organic" blocking means the Director will provide a framework and let the actors explore within it, and set the staging based on what comes out of that exploration. For example, the Director will provide the guideline that an actor needs to get from point A to point B before a certain line, but it's up to the actor to find their way. The goal here is to create staging that feels more natural, as it comes from the actor's impulses, rather than the Director's instructions. Organic blocking becomes more complicated because it will constantly change until it is "set" or until the show is "frozen." Both of these terms mean that the show has landed where the Director wants and they are no longer making changes. The reality is that there will always be some variation, but the Stage Manager now has a standard to try to maintain. Usually finalizing blocking has multiple stages. At the end of a rehearsal day the goal should be to have set a version of the staging that has been worked on that day. This does not mean the staging is not going to change the next time you go back to the scene, but a record of what has been done on that day should exist, so that a week later, when you come back to the scene, there is something to remind everyone what was done the last time. Because the cast and Director are actively living in the moment, maintaining an accurate record of what has been done becomes incredibly important so that the Stage Manager can communicate back to them what they just did. If a rehearsal is going well, the actors are likely not paying attention to what they are doing physically and so the Stage Manager's notation becomes invaluable in recreating elements of a performance that everyone likes.

The natural question with all of this is "How do you write down what movements people are doing?" Things change quickly in the rehearsal room and it is necessary to be able to write things down at the speed of other people's thoughts. Most union contracts will restrict the Stage Manager from making a video recording of a rehearsal, so the Stage Manager needs to be able to write quickly as they watch what's going on. This is where "blocking notation" comes into play. Blocking notation refers to the Stage Manager's shorthand for writing out the staging for a show. One of the great positives about blocking notation is that there is no universal standard. There is no requirement to learn another language but, rather, each person can develop what works best for them. One of the downsides to there not being a universal standard to all notation is that a way for other people to decipher the notation is going to need to be provided. This means creating a key that goes in front of the blocking script to help in that endeavor. All of this being said, there are a few abbreviations that are so common that they have essentially become industry standards:

Standard blocking key

SR = Stage Right

SL = Stage Left

USR = Upstage Right

DSR = Downstage Right

USL = Upstage Left

DSL = Downstage Left

CC = Center Center

X = Cross

Half the battle in establishing a method for taking blocking that works for you is to figure out how to set up the script. Stage Managers are different in how they approach this. Ideally this should be done in the cleanest way possible, because this script will become an integral part of the show's archive. The archive exists to both assist the team working on the current production to track what has been decided, and also to provide a reference should the production ever be mounted again. The simplest way to set up the script, and what is most common for theatre Stage Managers, is to simply make a note in the margins of the pages. As long as the handwriting is neat and the page is laid out in a clean way this can work very well.

The next version, which is slightly more work but a bit cleaner and more professional looking, is to create a lined sheet that goes on the opposite side of the script page where the notation is written out on one line and indicated in the corresponding location in the script with the line number.

The third, and most comprehensive version, is to create what are called "minis". Minis are simple miniature ground plans that are laid out on the lined blocking sheet and basically work the same way as version number two. This method layers on the detail of a hand-drawn picture to support the symbol notation. Any of these versions of laying out the blocking are totally valid and acceptable. It really comes down to the personal preferences of the Stage Manager and the expectation of the producer who is going to be receiving the book. Examples of these various techniques can be found on the Companion Website to this book.

Most of the time, in theatre, the production is not going to be remounted in exactly the same way, so the books become a part of the show's archive. In the opera world, however, where blocking is maintained by the Assistant Director, blocking scripts are of paramount importance because the industry relies on the renting and remounting of standing productions. In these cases, the original blocking notation can be in circulation for decades.

Making the rehearsal room work

Over the course of the rehearsal period the show is built piece by piece, with the ultimate goal of being able to run the entire show, sans scenery and costumes, in a fluid way. Stage management is usually on their own to make this happen. That team is the only one who will be in the rehearsal room to move props, furniture, or do whatever else needs to be done to be able to run the show smoothly. The benefit of this is that they get to know the show inside and out, in a hands-on way. This helps when they're bringing crew members up to speed in the theatre. However, this can get complicated if the show has a lot going on. Determining with the Director what the expectations are for how things will run in the room is wise before starting to try to run the show. If there are certain scene changes or complicated handoffs that you think will cause delays or hang-ups when running in the room, communicating those in advance will help alleviate any frustrations that might arise when those points are reached in a rehearsal. No matter how much you try to mitigate frustrations, the best way to ensure a smooth rehearsal is your own ingenuity. At the end of the day, the stage management team has the autonomy to do what they need to make the room function in as seamless a way as possible. They are there to support the artistic process and everyone in the room and, therefore, they can do what is needed to make that happen successfully.

The need to creatively problem-solve for unanticipated needs is going to come up frequently. This is especially common in organic staging processes. Someone will have a great idea and in order to flesh that idea out they will need a prop that has not been planned for, or a piece of furniture that is not currently available. The first person they will look to when these unplanned moments of brilliance strike will be the Stage Manager. These moments will give the SM the opportunity to stretch their creative muscles, and while some Stage Managers embrace these challenges others find them frustrating. Either way, someone on the team will need to come up with something. These "mockups" can be as simple as giving an actor a water bottle to use as a microphone, or as complex as building a rough version of the prop that is needed. It is a rare occurrence that the Stage Manager is left responsible for building a special prop, but it is certainly possible and becomes less rare when working in smaller theatre companies with less resources. It is not uncommon for Stage Managers to bring things in from home or to run out to source a simple prop item if they can get away. For example, if a teapot is needed and the SM happens to have one, and is comfortable bringing it to rehearsal, it will be much appreciated by everyone in the room. This rehearsal teapot may not be the final version that is used for the show, and may only be needed for a day before it gets cut, but the Stage Manager's resourcefulness has been able to keep the process moving. People often dedicate jackets or scarfs in the same way.

It is important to remember that being resourceful is a part of the job but offering personal belongings is not. These kinds of instances come down to personal comfort level. Never forget that there is a line between what the Stage Manager *has* to do and what they are *willing* to do. Drawing clear lines and boundaries for yourself is only going to help maintain a positive outlook on the job. When people allow themselves to be placed in situations that make them frustrated or uncomfortable, they will only become progressively more discontented with their work environment and that will bleed into their job performance.

Rehearsal reports

During the course of any rehearsal there's a lot of information that comes up. Some of it is going to be rehashing already discussed topics, while others will be slight or even dramatic changes. For example, if the plan has always been for an actor to sit in a chair but it becomes clear during rehearsal that they need a stool, the Stage Manager could easily email or text the appropriate person to let them know so they source the correct item. However, when notes and changes begin to mount at a fast pace, consolidating them makes sense. Communicating these changes widely is also critical as, if they are significant, they may impact multiple people in multiple departments. In order to make the Stage Manager and everyone else's lives a little easier, the rehearsal report was developed. These are exactly what they sound like; a report of the activities of the day and any notes that may have arisen during the course of the rehearsal. These documents come in many different formats and each Stage Manager has a form they prefer. Sometimes a company will dictate the format they would like used but this is rare, and it is normally left to the Stage Manager to figure out the clearest method of communication.

While the format may vary, the elements of the report are universal.

- Title of show
- Date of rehearsal
- Director name
- Stage Manager name
- Schedule of the day: This is the schedule of what actually happened during the course of the rehearsal. The rehearsal schedule for the day (which was previously distributed) included the plan, but this should be a record of how the day actually played out. The schedule that is included in the rehearsal report should detail how time was used in the room,

when breaks were taken, what scenes were completed, and what time the cast was released. There are a few uses for this information. First, it helps the Stage Manager keep a record of what has actually been accomplished. There are going to be days where the Director doesn't complete everything that was planned, when working on complicated shows with lots of small individual scenes it can become difficult to keep track of what hasn't been done or what needs some time dedicated to touch it up.

Second, it serves as an important archival tool for the Producers to understand what's happening in the room. Sometimes looking at how time is used is more telling than getting verbal feedback about the way that rehearsal is going. It can also serve as a safety record for the Stage Manager with the union. Identifying when breaks were taken is going to be really useful in the event that someone says rules are not being followed. Creating a paper trail using the rehearsal reports can prove that things are running correctly and serve as a protection for the SM.

- Summary of rehearsal: This is just a brief two- or three-sentence summary of how things are going. Let the schedule and department notes speak for themselves. This should not be a long narrative description of everything that happened during the rehearsal, but rather is about morale. It's a great way to communicate to producers, in a very public way, how everyone seems to be doing. Keep in mind that these reports have a wide distribution so carefully choosing the language that is used in the summary is important. Most of the report features cold, factual reporting, but the summary articulates the Stage Manager's opinion of what is going on and so being overly negative or offensive could come back to bite them. Some Stage Managers hate doing the summary because it tends to feel disingenuous, and they would not be wrong, but there is a difference between lying and being tactful.

Let's say that things are going very well in your rehearsal process. You can quite honestly say: "Today was another wonderful day of rehearsal. We accomplished everything we set out to and are looking forward to another great day tomorrow." This may sound overly cheery to some people but is an honest description of a very positive rehearsal day. Now let's say things are not going so well. The cast and Director are struggling to get along and things are moving very slowly, leading you to not complete everything you had laid out for the day. How do you articulate that in the summary without it being disingenuous but still being polite and professional? Something along the lines of "Despite some challenges during the course of the day, we were able to accomplish quite a bit. We continue to move forward and while we were not able to accomplish everything today, we do have a plan of how to pick things up starting tomorrow," makes it clear that there's a little bit of unrest in the room, but it doesn't go into a lot of detail about it. It tells the Producers enough that they may give you a call to figure out what's going on. It also honestly communicates the fact that, though we didn't get to everything, we have a plan moving forward.

The rehearsal reports serve as both a communication tool and a paper trail for the production. In going back and looking at the reports, you can see exactly how a show progressed and developed over time. It also allows a very busy creative and production team to have a document that they are able to reference to be sure nothing has been missed or forgotten. Every theatrical process produces a lot of paper but the rehearsal reports are one of the most important. They are also, unfortunately, one of the least read. There are always a few people in every process who just never read the rehearsal reports. It is a frustrating reality, but it should not discourage the SM from creating them. They are critically important to the health of the process and their absence is always missed when they are not provided in a consistent and comprehensive manner.

The final days

No matter what length of time has been spent in a rehearsal room, the last few days often feel like a mad dash for the stage management team. They now have their feet firmly planted in two separate parts of the process as they try to effectively wrap up the room rehearsals and prepare to move to stage. This split can be hard to manage and can often necessitate splitting the team up to manage it properly. While the Stage Manager focuses on guiding the room through the last few days in the room, the ASMs are often frantically putting the final touches on the running paperwork that will make the transition to the stage, and the introduction of the crew, as smooth as possible.

These last days are usually marked by trying to get through a complete run-through of the show and ensuring the cast feels comfortable with everything that is expected of them before the focus shifts away from them as tech begins. These final run-throughs are critically important for the creative team to understand how the fully realized version of the show will differ from what was merely conceptual before. With any luck, the creative team will be able to attend at least one run of each act so that they are able to visualize the things that have only been discussed in the reports each night. The Director and Stage Manager will usually designate a specific room run as the "designer run," where the design team is formally invited to attend. Depending on the way in which the Director prefers to work, and how much rehearsal time you actually have, there may be an open-door policy for designers to attend any rehearsal, but it is helpful to set a specific date so that everyone is on the same page and those in the room can design the rehearsals to be ready for that targeted moment. There is also the possibility crew members may attend this run-through. Because they have the most direct interaction with the actors and their staging, it is most common for only the wardrobe and wig and makeup supervisors to attend, but if the show is sufficiently complicated it is not totally unheard of to have other departments there as well.

As the Stage Managers prepare to move to the stage they will kick into full archive mode. It is going to save everyone many headaches to have a record of as much of what worked in the rehearsal room as possible. The first, and maybe most important, piece of the physical archiving of the room is the measuring of spike marks. A spike mark is a piece of tape that indicates the position of a piece of furniture, prop, or person. These marks are separate from the taped-out set lines on the floor. The measurements of the spikes can be plotted out in the same way the floor was originally taped out; measure upstage and over from center. Use your best judgment as you archive the room. If significant scaling adjustments had to be made to tape out the set in the room, the spikes may not be as relevant so approximating the positions on stage may be reasonable. This is also true if a piece has been, and will continue to be, moved around. Don't allow the team to get too heavily bogged down in the measuring of spikes and identify what is important and what is not before starting.

Again, the Stage Managers, as much as possible, should use room rehearsals to sort out what the running of backstage will be like. Hopefully, by the end of the rehearsal process they will have figured out a prop table setup that makes sense for the show and for the actors, so taking pictures of that layout to more easily replicate it on stage is a great idea. There are even times where the same tables can be used and the team simply needs to label it and move it to the stage with them. The same goes for any quick-change plans that may have been figured out in the room and any onstage prop presets as well. The more that can be taken from what was learned in the room and directly transferred to the stage, the smoother the tech rehearsal process will be.

As is obvious, the magic word for the final days in the rehearsal room is "archive." Being specific and comprehensive during the archiving of the information learned in the rehearsal room is critical to a successful transition to the stage. This is, of course, the ideal. The reality, however, is that the stage management team is going to find themselves incredibly busy just trying to manage the rehearsal actively happening, that finding time to archive is going to be challenging. This is why it is important to start recording this information from the beginning. During the prep period, put together the running paperwork templates so that there is something to start filling in on the first day of rehearsal. The more diligent everyone is in their note-taking early in the process, when the Director is moving slowly through the show, the easier it is to simply update those older notes as the pace quickens.

Everyone has a favorite part of the process of putting a production together. For some Stage Managers, room rehearsals make all the work worthwhile. The sense of collaboration and camaraderie that develops during rehearsals can lead to some of the most fun you will have during the entire run of a show. Tech tends to be stressful and time to spend getting to know each other can be tight. Once a show opens everyone is only together for performances, so downtime for bonding is more scarce. What is lovely about rehearsals is the opportunity to hang out and develop relationships with colleagues in what is hopefully a lower-pressure environment. Take advantage of that part of the experience, both personally and professionally. It is a great opportunity to develop wonderful friendships and also future working relationships. Remember, it's all about who you know.

4

Technical Rehearsals

The next phase of the process of getting a show in front of an audience is technical, or "tech," rehearsals. This is the moment when the technical elements, which have been missing from room rehearsals, are finally introduced. The full set, props, lighting, sound, and costumes come together for the first time in a new wave of rehearsals that put the focus on getting those elements finalized, and integrating them with the staging that has been established. During this much shorter rehearsal period, the creative team will get a look at what the final product will be, and how the original concepts need to be tweaked now that they exist in the real world. This part of the process is also probably the most stressful for the Stage Manager.

Stage Managers are charged with integrating the hypothetical work that was done in the room with the reality of what exists on stage in a safe and efficient way. For weeks, the Stage Manager may have been calling out that scenery is moving during a certain scene, but now there is a 30-foot wall flying in from above that can seriously injure someone if they are not paying attention. After all the planning and copious amounts of communication, everyone will look to the Stage Manager to facilitate making all of the elements work together cohesively. This is where taking the time to get to know your colleagues and building a strong bond of trust is going to pay off. The Stage Manager is also going to be leading the charge as a large number of new people are added into the production. There will now be a full crew, with members from every different department, who know nothing about what is happening in the show and need to be brought up to speed very quickly. It is in the incorporating of the crew where the stage management team's ability to communicate, both verbally and on paper, will truly be tested. Despite the stresses and challenges associated with the technical rehearsal process, the chance to finally see things come together and execute the planning they have done up until now is one of the most exciting parts of mounting a show for the stage management team.

Getting the stage ready

Prior to actually moving into the theater space for rehearsals with the cast, it is wise for the stage management team to visit and get the lay of the land. The cast has been working on a flat floor, with only colored tape to reference, and now they will need to deal with the physical reality of not only the set but the architecture of the theater itself. Part of the Stage Manager's responsibility is to prepare the space in advance, to mitigate some of the shell shock and inherent dangers associated with adding a whole new physical world.

Sets invariably come with step-ups, trip hazards, loose nails, exposed screws, and any number of potentially injury-causing issues. While the load in crew, Technical Director, and Production Manager will all try to make the space as safe as possible, it's important for the stage management team to request a walk-through before tech begins. Even if this has to occur the morning of the first day of tech, it is critical to get in the space so that any problems can be flagged in advance and fixed, if possible. It also will allow stage management time to determine how to course correct for any issues that cannot be fixed prior to the cast stepping on stage.

What to watch out for

- *"What is the cast's route from dressing room to stage?"*
  One of the easiest ways to create a smooth start to tech is to make the cast feel comfortable in the building from the moment they walk in. The best way to accomplish this is to ensure they don't feel lost right away. During the walk-through look out for the best route for the cast to get from the entrance to their dressing rooms, and from their rooms to the stage. Identify whether signage needs to be hung or if it already exists for this purpose. Some theaters will even provide a representative who will greet the cast to direct them. If there are Production Assistants on the stage management team, the Stage Manager can also delegate greeter duties to them, if they can be spared from the work on stage.

  Helpful hint: Most venues will require all signs be hung using blue painter's tape to protect their walls so having some in the Stage Manager's kit is always wise.

- *Safety first*

  This was alluded to before, but walk the set carefully and think through all the things that could potentially cause a problem once rehearsal begins. Identify where there are edges to the scenery that someone might bump into in the dark. Look out for any small lips in the seams on the floor or stairs that might create a trip hazard. Carefully check the reverse of scenery for any exposed screws. These are often the hardest to find but can do the most damage. Pay attention to areas that cast will interact with and don't worry about screws in areas of the set that a cast member would be unable to reach. As areas of concern become apparent, communicate with the Technical Director, or Crew Head, so that anything that can be fixed, will be. For anything that is not fixable, glow- or white-taping them is the most common way to attract people's attention. For any backstage areas, do not be afraid to be liberal in the use of tape to ensure that all potentially dangerous hazards are made obvious. On stage, any safety taping should be done carefully and subtly so as not to draw the audience's attention. The goal here should be to proactively address any concerns the cast might have when they arrive. It is likely that they will discover something that has been missed but seeing that the stage management team has been diligent in trying to protect their safety will only instill more confidence in the team's abilities. Remember, the stage management team should know the show better than anyone else. This means that their eyes on the stage space will be invaluable to making sure everything is ready for the cast.

  Helpful hint: Glow tape only works when it has been "charged" by being exposed to light for a period of time, immediately before the lights go out. If you plan to use it, be cognizant of what the lighting conditions are in the area you will place it. If it is going in a corner that does not get much illumination, placing white tape may be your best bet to call attention to the issue.

- *Scope out your territory*

  At the end of the day, the only person looking out for the Stage Manager is the Stage Manager themselves. As the technical rehearsals are as much for the Stage Manager as for anyone else, it is critical that they have the facilities they need to do their job. Once issues regarding safety are well in hand, the Stage Managers should investigate their own positions, both for tech and the performance. ASMs should walk the backstage area and ask "Where am I going to be for this show?" The room rehearsals will have provided a lot of guidance on where ASMs will need to be at any given moment but, just like the cast, the ASM is now dealing with the physical reality of walls, lighting positions, and other elements that may create visual obstructions that were not present before. Take the time to figure out the best way to run the show and do not be afraid to ask for things you need. Many ASMs will simply ask for a music stand to keep their script on, but different shows and different people need different things, so try to think comprehensively about the production and try to prepare the backstage area in a way that sets everyone up for success.

Stage Managers should always stake out their claim to tech table space upon arrival. Various people will want to sit near or at the tech table but, again, this is a rehearsal for the Stage Manager and creative team so they must have priority. The layout of the table will be a negotiation with the Lighting Designer and programmer, if you are sharing. Many Stage Managers prefer to sit on the end of the table so that they have easier access to hop up and move about the theater as needed. At the end of the day, however, it's a personal preference, and what works best for communication during the tech process should win out. More and more theaters have begun to provide a separate table for the Stage Manager. This is always a lovely luxury to have but is not something that can be counted on. In addition to staking out their own space at the table, it is always worth the Stage Manager checking that everything that is required has been set up on the tech tables. The biggest item being communications or "com." The tech table headsets should be in place from the moment the Lighting Designer walks in the door as they will, invariably, want to get to work with the programmer at once. Often they will light over whatever onstage work needs to be addressed. It is also wise to hop on headset to check that everything is in full working order. One of the worst and most frustrating moments in tech is being about to get started and finding out that no one can hear you.

As much as possible, the Stage Manager should carve out time to ensure that they have what they need to be successful. It can be hard to do as the team prepares everything for the cast's arrival, but neglecting the needs of the stage management team can have an incredibly detrimental effect on the process as a whole. To reiterate, the Stage Managers must look out for themselves, so find the time.

Arrivals

As time gets closer to the start of the rehearsal, more and more of the team from the rehearsal room will begin to appear at the theater. Some will have been there before and some will be brand new to the space. Either way, people want to feel welcomed as they arrive. There is a certain amount of natural anxiety that exists around the tech process and some of that can be alleviated by a friendly, familiar face. While it is not a requirement, it is always nice to have someone from stage management available to the cast and creative team as they arrive. This does not mean that they need to stand by the door to greet people, but identifying someone on the team whose job it will be to answer questions and provide some guidance will go a long way toward setting a positive tone for the tech process. There's almost no doubt that at least one or two cast members will wander into the building from the wrong entrance or will not see the signage that has been posted and will need some level of guidance around the building. Assigning a member of the team to this duty can help to mitigate some of the confusion and frustration being in a new place can cause.

All the preparatory work that was discussed earlier will hopefully be complete by the time the arrivals begin, but if it is not, make sure everyone on your team, (especially whoever is going to be greeting the cast) is aware. Purely from a safety perspective it is important that no one in the cast has access to the stage until the Stage Manager has given them the all clear. This can be communicated verbally before leaving the rehearsal room and should be reiterated in writing via email and even posted backstage. Everyone is always very anxious to get on stage and walk around, to get a sense of the space, but stage management as a team will need to run defense to ensure that everyone remains safe, and that no one unwittingly puts themselves in harms way. In addition to ensuring people are staying clear of off-limits areas, stage management will also need to keep track to make sure people are where they need to be at any given moment. Depending on the type of show, cast members may need to report for costume fittings, makeup calls, or simply to get into microphones. So much is integrated at once during the tech process, it is critical that the Stage Manager is keeping everyone on track when it comes to the schedule. This may mean diverting creative team members and cast to various locations to prepare for the rehearsal rather than allowing them to explore the space, as they likely will want to do. Again, assigning someone from the team to run point on the arrivals process can make life much easier for all the Stage Managers on a show.

Calling the show

Any time spent around Stage Managers will invariably lead to a conversation about "calling" the show. Calling the show refers to verbally communicating to the crew when technical cues are to be taken during a live performance. Anything on stage that needs guidance by the Stage Manager in performance is a viable thing that could be called. The Stage Manager's primary role during a performance is to ensure that the show the audience sees is the same show the Director intended. During tech, their ultimate goal is to make sure that the technical elements are smoothly integrated with what was established in the rehearsal room. While the Director may be the one who has the vision for the final show, it is the Stage Manager who makes it happen in front of an audience.

The Stage Manager holds the artistic intention of every designer, the timing of every cue, and the artistic ideology of what a production is trying to achieve in their brain. They need to be able to synthesize all of that information and clearly and coherently communicate it to a crew, who executes the show in front of a live audience. The Stage Manager functions as a conductor, and the technical elements are their orchestra. In any orchestra every musician knows what they're supposed to be doing but cannot play independently and still hope that it will sound good. They require a conductor to set the tempo, keep them on track, and cue them appropriately. If something goes wrong and a section of the orchestra falls behind, it is the conductor who must get them back on track. There is a direct equivalency between those responsibilities of a conductor during a concert and the responsibilities a Stage Manager takes on when they call the show.

The calling script

The Stage Manager, up until now, has been maintaining the prompt book, which contains all blocking notation and record of what has been accomplished on the show as it heads into tech. The Stage Manager's prompt book is the key element of the show's archive and is the guiding record for transitioning the show from the rehearsal space to the stage. The next layer of information that is added to this record are the technical cues and how they are placed within the script.

Different Stage Managers will organize this in different ways. Some will simply add these cues to the existing blocking script. The benefit of this method is that all information is consolidated to a single document that will be comprehensive. The downside is that, often, blocking scripts can get messy, and the notes on the staging will take up a significant amount of space on each page. This means that in adding cue placements and notes it can become difficult to decipher what is needed to call the show and what is not. Having so much information on a page can be what leads to missed cues or a messy script.

The second method is to get a clean copy of the script and make a single, dedicated calling script. This clearly will eliminate the problem of too much unnecessary information on a single page, but it does require reference to a separate document should a question of blocking arise. Usually, when choosing to go down this route any staging notes that are pertinent to the calling of the show will need to be copied over, otherwise the script will be devoid of staging details and extraneous information.

Whatever method is chosen, the most critical purpose of the calling script is that it is readable by somebody else. This is true for all stage management paperwork, but most especially for the calling script. Stage Managers often feel a very personal ownership over their calling scripts and, while that can be helpful as they prepare it for their own use, it is important to remember the "hit-by-a-bus" rule. If something were to happen to the Stage Manager, can an ASM or outside Stage Manager walk in the door, pick up the script, and call the show almost flawlessly? This is an intense standard to live up to but is a critical goal to strive for. The old adage of "the show must go on" is embraced across all theatrical disciplines, but the show cannot go on without the Stage Manager and that person is human. Stage Managers can fall ill, have family crises, or have unexpected life issues that pull them away, so there is always the possibility that someone else will have to pick up the book and use it.

Creating something that is universally readable is a difficult prospect, but by the time the calling script is being assembled the Stage Manager should have the tools needed to accomplish it. The real challenge is just making sure that things are articulated in a clear and concise manner that someone else can understand. During the tech process a lot of information is flying around very quickly and it will be natural to jot down notes that only the Stage Manager will understand. The key is to carve out time once things calm down to go back over those notes and clean them up in a systematic way. Waiting too long to do this will most likely lead to not doing it at all. It can be very easy to get complacent with the calling script, and many Stage Managers feel a great deal of anxiety when confronted with the notion of editing their notes once they have called the show successfully for the first time. One of the most common superstitions among Stage Managers is that once the show has been called well, touching the book will lead to a disaster in the next go around. To combat this anxiety, some Stage Managers will dedicate time at the end of the performance process to clean up their book so that it is usable as an archive for future mountings of the production. While this is an excellent thing to do, it does not solve the problem of "What if something happens during the run?" Cleaning the book incrementally throughout the tech process and immediately following opening will provide a cleaner version to call from and an excellent resource should someone other than the Stage Manager have to call the show.

The art of the call

It is almost universally accepted that calling the show is the most obvious and visible example of the artistic contribution of the Stage Manager. Throughout weeks of meetings, rehearsals, side conversations, and emails, the Stage Manager accumulates a massive amount of information from the creative and production teams that all needs to be synthesized to create a cohesive show. It is the responsibility of the Stage Manager to take those disparate parts, which are all hoping to work together, and make them a seamless theatrical experience when the house lights go down.

The first, and most important thing, to know about calling a show is that almost nothing occurs on stage without the Stage Manager saying "GO." This single rule is the key to a good performance and also the most anxiety-inducing part of being the show caller. Everyone from the crew to the cast needs to remember this fundamental rule, simply because as the "conductor" of the performance the SM has to have ultimate control of what is happening. The idea is that the Stage Manager is the keeper of the singular vision of what the audience is meant to see and experience. This is one of the reasons building a strong foundation of trust with everyone is so key to success as a Stage Manager. Everyone on the creative team has to be confident in that person's ability to accurately and sensitively execute his or her intended vision. Producers have to trust that they can provide their audiences with the experience that they are paying for. Everyone makes mistakes, and human error is forgivable, but a lack of calling ability or respect for the work can be a clear sign that the person is in the wrong industry.

Putting the control of the pacing of a performance in the hands of a Stage Manager allows all departments to rely on a single voice controlling all things as one. If something goes wrong, the Stage Manager is hopefully going to be able to evaluate the situation and make a decision on how to proceed, so that everyone is working towards a single goal as they try to keep the show moving. Without a clearly defined leader in a situation like this, there is a high level of risk that the problem will be exacerbated by numerous voices all fighting to fix the problem. In a high-pressure and time-sensitive situation having numerous people working towards individual goals can lead to a muddled solution or even an unsafe situation as things get missed. By consolidating control, the team can be unified by the single voice cutting through the din.

Clearly, the Stage Manager wields enormous amounts of power and responsibility when calling a show. Being the central, not sole, person responsible for the safety of the cast and the correct execution of the show, clarity and specificity in the way in which the Stage Manager calls shows becomes critical. Consistency in the way in which cues are called, and the timing of those calls, allows crew members to know what to expect and to not be caught off guard. There is an industrywide expectation that the Stage Manager projects a calm and restrained demeanor as they call a show. This doesn't mean that they need to aim for a lack of humor or personality, but ensuring there is an evenness to the tone of their voice and a composure to the way things are articulated sets everyone at ease and instills confidence and focus.

Show-calling vocabulary and structure

- *Warning*: To "warn" someone is to provide advance notice that a cue is forthcoming. Warnings are usually given about five minutes prior to the cue being called and are often lumped together in groups; for example, "This is a warning on light cues 47–63, sound cues 12 and 13, and rail cue 5." Warnings are often viewed as optional and usually are utilized in instances where there are long breaks between cues for any department. This can happen quite frequently in plays where once a scene begins there may be no technical changes until the scene ends.
- *Standby*: Standbys are a requirement. Like warnings, they provide advance notice that a cue is coming up. Standbys are normally given anywhere from thirty seconds to two minutes prior to a cue being

called. A standby is meant to signal the crew that they should get into position to execute the cue. For this reason, it is important not to give standbys too early. When there is a piece of scenery that is going to fly in, a standby tells the flyman that they should unlock the rope and have their hands on it, ready to pull. There is no reason to have the rope unlocked for a prolonged period of time, and doing so only increases the likelihood of a mistake being made.

- *GO*: The word "Go" is the magic word that everyone in the theatre recognizes as the command for something to happen. No crew member should take a cue without hearing the Stage Manager say "Go" and it is important that that rule is enforced. It is always great to have a light board operator cover you and take cues that you might miss or call incorrectly, but that kind of action needs to be tempered. It is important to ensure that action is only taken from the Stage Manager's "Go" as they are the one who is ultimately responsible for the performance. It can also cause safety concerns if a crew member goes rogue, as they have the potential to not have the big picture of the show in mind in the same way as stage management. It is not uncommon for people in a theater to never use the world "Go" in casual conversation, but rather spell out "G-O" just to be safe. This is a bit of theatre superstition but also reinforces how sacred the word is.

In addition to being consistent in the vocabulary that is used to call a show, the Stage Manager needs to be consistent in the way that they structure the cues. Very similar to correct grammar, is a specific sentence structure associated with calling cues for a performance.

For any preparatory cues:

> *Warning + Department + "Cue" + Cue Number* (e.g., Warning Light Cue 7)
> *Standby + Department + "Cue" + Cue Number* (e.g., Standby Light Cue 7)

For actual cue execution:

> *Department + "Cue" + Cue Number + "GO"* (e.g., Light Cue 7 GO)

As is outlined in the above examples, one of the critical elements to maintaining clarity as a show is called is the inclusion of both the cue number and the department who will be executing it. With multiple crews that are waiting for cues from the Stage Manager, it is important to call out the department that is being spoken to directly. Many Stage Managers will abbreviate their calls to include only the cue number and will drop the department. There are certain instances where abbreviating in this way makes sense, but those are few, and no matter what, not calling out the department opens the door for the wrong person to take a cue. Another failsafe against accidently cueing the wrong person is the actual cue names themselves. Some designers will use letters rather than numbers to label their cues. This is not very common but is certainly not unheard of and does help to differentiate cues to protect against an operator mishearing what department the Stage Manager has called out and taking their cue at the wrong moment.

Maintaining a consistent structure in the way in which cues are spoken is going to help people follow them more accurately. If the structure is changed and the Stage Manager begins dropping bits of information, it becomes harder for the crew to follow them and anxiety begins to mount. Adding additional anxiety to the overall headset environment is not useful to anyone working on the show. Tone also goes a long way to keeping tensions low and helps to guide people as they follow the Stage Manager's lead. It's important to constantly convey a level of calm and confidence during the call. At no point should the Stage Manager sound frazzled or out of control. It's important that the voice coming from the Stage Manager feels like a solid anchor for everyone who is listening.

The final piece of the show-calling puzzle is timing. Obviously the Stage Manager helps to set the pace of the show in the calling of transitions and other technical moments that influence how the cast moves things along on stage. Beyond the artistic element of timing in show-calling, there is also a practical consideration. Colloquially it is called "back-timing." Once a Stage Manager knows where they need a cue to occur, they need to back-time the calling of that cue to make sure it happens at the right moment. There are two phases to this process. The first it to determine how long it takes the board operator to actually hit the GO button. The Stage Manager needs to be sure that the word "GO" comes out of their mouth in just enough time for the operator to hit the button at the right second. This means calling the GO a split second before the cue is meant to actually occur. The second facet of back-timing is ensuring that you have enough time to get all the words you need to speak out of your mouth so that the "GO" is timed to allow the cue to be executed correctly. In order to get all the words out it is important to use abbreviations and shorthand wherever possible, but clarity will remain key and is not expendable. This means that there may be times where the Stage Manager has to say absolutely everything related to the cue sequence in order to get it to happen correctly. All of this sounds very complicated but it becomes instinctual with time. It is likely that after a few shows a Stage Manager has no need to consciously break all of this down and can just feel the rapport with the board operators, but every once in a while there will be people who do not connect and a more technical approach to back-timing may be required.

Integrating the crew

In addition to all of the physical puzzle pieces that are being added to a production during the tech process, there is also a significant number of staff that have not been a part of the rehearsals up until now. It's not until tech rehearsals start that the crew joins the team. The term "crew" is a very general moniker for Stagehands, Electricians, props people, Sound Engineers, Riggers, Dressers, Makeup Artists, Scenic Painters, and anyone else that is going to participate in the physical running of the show. While the Stage Manager will be seated in the booth playing air traffic controller, the crew are the people who are flying the planes. Every theater is set up differently. In a very small nonunion theater it is not uncommon for the Stage Manager to also serve as the light and sound board operator. Due to the physical constraints of needing to be near the boards, it is less common for the Stage Manager to participate in scene changes but it is not unheard of. Many young Stage Managers begin their careers working in the kinds of situations where they are the one pressing the GO button. Larger organizations that can afford the appropriate staffing will add more and more people to the team and the crew will grow larger and larger. The more complicated the show, the more people involved. In a union crew setting, the Stage Manager is not allowed to touch anything, so an ability to clearly communicate is critical.

The crew, like the creative team, is broken up into individual departments. Each department has a very specific specialty and, in the union world, there is minimal crossover between the various departments. While an individual may be put on different crews for different calls, they will rarely move to another crew during a single call.

- *Stagehand*: The general term that most often refers to members of either the carpentry or prop crews. Carpenters are closely associated with scenery. That means if there are walls that need to move or large rolling units that need to be set, the Carps will be the ones to handle those items. They will also assist with minor repairs and adjustments that may occur during the course of a run. Carpenters also tend to maintain certain elements of the physical stage space itself. If the stage floor has a crack, for example, the Carps will likely address it, at least until it can be fixed by the venue staff. The props crew will handle all hand props, furniture, some small scenic units, and other items that are deemed to fall under their purview. The props department is also usually charged with sweeping and mopping the stage. As with Scenic Designers and Prop Masters, there is a certain amount of debate between Carps and Props as to what items belong to which crew. Once that distinction has been settled it is important for the stage management team to honor it and know who to go to for what.

- *Wardrobe*: The next department that stage management has the most direct contact with, after Props and Carps, is Wardrobe. The wardrobe team members are referred to individually as Dressers. Dressers will maintain the garments and organize them to make sure that the appropriate garment gets to the correct actor during the course of the tech process and run of show. Dressers will assist the cast with quick changes and with getting people in and out of complicated costumes. Please remember that the department is referred to as "wardrobe." A Costume Designer will generate "costumes," which are the physical garments that the cast members will wear. There is a wardrobe department comprised of Dressers who are responsible for actually running the show and maintaining the costumes. Understanding and utilizing the correct terminology shows a degree of respect for the crew and will help to build a more positive relationship with these new members of the shows community.

- *Wigs and makeup*: The wigs and makeup department is comprised of makeup artists and hairstylists. Depending on the complexity of the show, wig or prosthetic specialists my also be brought in to supplement the hair and makeup department. Often you will hear these two departments, along with wardrobe, lumped together as one. This is due to the dramatic overlap and collaboration that exists between them. Wardrobe, wigs, and makeup have as close a (if not closer) relationship as Props and Carps. Often all of these departments will be involved in a quick change and so the members of each will need to work in tandem to accomplish the changes. The Wig and Makeup Artists will maintain the wigs for a show and execute the Designer's vision for the cast.

- *Electrics*: The electrics department will handle all lighting and power needs for a show. Depending on the complexity of the show the Stage Manager may have very little interaction with the electrics department. Often this particular crew is large in the days leading up to tech, as the light plot is loaded in, but once everything is set it will drop down dramatically. The run crew for electrics is usually one of the smallest on a show, comprised of the Light Board Operator and a Deck Electrician, with Spot Operators if needed. As with all of the crews, the scale of the show will determine the size of the crew. The one member of electrics that the Stage Manager is guaranteed to have a lot of interaction with is the Light Board Operator. As previously stated, there are situations where the Stage Manager may be called upon to press the GO button on the light board, but in most theatrical settings, there will be a dedicated operator whose job it is to sit at the board and press GO. The board op is going to be the resident expert on the programming for the show. They will monitor the status of all lights and assist the Stage Manager in ensuring that the design doesn't start to degrade. The board op has eyes on the monitors at the light board and can provide any information the Stage Manager may require on the status of cues and instruments. This means that if, while calling a tech rehearsal, the Stage Manager has a question about how long a cue takes to complete, the board op is able to provide that information instantly.

- *Audio*: Audio is the last major department that the Stage Manager will interact with on a regular basis. In addition to the obvious management of speakers, sound cues, microphones, etc., the sound department also generally deals with headsets within the theater. In most houses the sound department is also responsible for video. As the inclusion of video content via projection, LED walls, etc., are becoming more prevalent in the theatre, there is a greater push for specialization in this area on crews. For the time being, however, video falls under the umbrella of the audio department. On a simple play with no amplification and just a few sound cues there may only be a board operator, who will be taking the cues as you call them and maintaining the system to ensure that everything is functional at all times. On a musical there will be a Sound Engineer, front of house, who is going to be mixing the amplification of the show. There will also be a team of A2s backstage. A2s are responsible for the physical microphones and function as the sound-running crew to ensure that the mics are on, and they will handle any problems that may arise. This deck crew can expand depending on the needs of the show. A standard musical is likely to be mixed by a single person with one to two A2s backstage. A larger, more intricate show that includes a large orchestra may have multiple people working at the soundboard. Depending on the complexity of the show and the size of the venue there may even be a "score reader" by the board with the mixer. This person will follow along with the show's script or score, and verbally call out which microphones need to be turned on and when to the Sound Engineer. This frees the engineer to be able to keep their eyes on the board and keep their focus on listening to how things sound in the house. In the same way that electricity is a topic that many people that are not involved in that world do not understand, sound is another thing that many Stage Managers, unless they have experience in it, may not have any detailed knowledge of. To a certain extent, not understanding every nuance is okay. Most can get by but should take the time to gain some understanding of the component parts of the work people are doing. Talk to a Sound Engineer and begin to try and gain some level of understanding of the elements of a microphone, for example. This way, if there is a crackling or a mic is going in and out during a show, the Stage Manager won't feel completely at sea and can help solve the problem, rather than wait on others to come up with something.

Developing an understanding of the responsibilities of each department will only go to show that the Stage Manager has respect for the work that each person is doing. This visible respect will help to develop a more collaborative and collegial relationship with the crew. There is a stereotype that exists for stagehands, particularly union ones, that they're grumpy or unpleasant, but while those people certainly are out there that is just a microcosm of all of the people doing these jobs. Just as there are unpleasant Stage Managers and unpleasant actors and unpleasant directors, these individuals are not representative of their entire field and it's important for Stage Managers, who often function as the liaison between creative teams and the crew, to dispel some of those stereotypes. What is most inspirational, frankly, is that those people who do have a grumpier personality are usually that way because they are deeply committed to the work that they're doing. In the same way that a Director's high standards may push them to behave in a way that many find difficult to deal with, a crew member may also have those same high standards.

Many on the crew love to talk about their history and careers, and those stories are some of the best available in the theatrical world. Count yourself lucky when you get to work with an amazing group of crew members because these people are just as invested in their work as you are in yours. They may show it differently, but they deserve the respect that is given to any other collaborator in the process. And they have no other defender with a creative team than the Stage Manager. Part of the Stage Manager's role is to be their champion, and while the Stage Manager doesn't have to agree with every decision they make, looking out for their well-being in the same way as looking out for the cast or the other Stage Managers is crucial, as they are also a part of the team that the Stage Manager is going to be managing for the run of a show.

The tech process can be tough for the Stage Manager, but there is a reason that many refer to it as their favorite part of the job. Getting to finally see things come together is incredibly exciting for everyone on a project, but for the Stage Manager this is their moment to shine. Through all the stress and trials associated with this portion of the process the Stage Manager must remain a steady rudder and drive things forward. "Driving the bus" can be tough but the culture of mutual respect and trust that was built during the room rehearsal period will finally pay off during tech. This is the moment to call in the favors, so to speak, and ask people to work together in a positive and enthusiastic way. The more the Stage Manager can project that confidence in their work and enthusiasm, the more it will filter out to the rest of the people they are working with. Tech can be tons of fun, but it is also the end of one era of the show. Rehearsals are over and a whole contingent of the team will be leaving. Once the show opens the creative team will all depart and the Stage Manager will be left to keep things moving for the remainder of the show's run. This departure and transition of responsibility will change the role of the Stage Manager dramatically.

5

Running the Show

After weeks and even months of buildup, opening night happens. From that moment on, the nature of the Stage Manager's role shifts dramatically, from one of technical support and logistics to one of artistic maintenance and general management. Traditionally, following opening night the Designers and Director will walk away, popping in from time to time during the run, but are essentially done with their work on the project. It is now in the hands of the Stage Manager to ensure that the audience is experiencing the production as intended at each performance. This is one of the main reasons why building a comprehensive and accurate archive of the show is critical during the rehearsal process. The Stage Manager now becomes the voice of the creative team for the cast, and having a hard record of what was done before is critical to fall back on.

Maintaining the show

Performing live in front of an audience day after day is naturally going to cause an evolution in the production. As cast and crew get more comfortable with the work they are doing, the initial pressure and stress to get it right will abate. This is not to say they no longer care, but a natural rhythm will develop and muscle memory will take over from attention to detail. This relaxation allows people to start discovering new ways of doing things. This can be how an actor approaches a line or how the crew organizes a scene change to make it more efficient. There is also an innate desire to change things up. Settling into the work can lead to complacency, and even boredom, so some people will actively look for new ways to approach their job on the show. All of this leads to incremental changes to the production that the Director and Designers had not intended for the audience to see. The fundamental difference between the Stage Manager's role during rehearsals and during the run of show is that they absorb the roles of the entire creative team and must try to fight back against this evolution. This is called "maintaining the show."

Show maintenance is the single biggest responsibility that the Stage Manager has after opening. This includes keeping an eye on every aspect of the production, from actors' performances to the look of a lighting cue. Essentially, all elements of a production coalesce under the Stage Manager's watchful eye after opening, and that can be a challenge for one person to be responsible for. You are, of course, working with a team of people who will let you know when a prop breaks or a costume is damaged and needs significant repair, but it is ultimately the Stage Manager who has to gauge the impact of any adjustment to the show and address it appropriately. There is a growing trend, especially in large for-profit theatre, to hire a resident director who would take much of the artistic responsibility from the Stage Manager's shoulders, but that change is not universal yet and the tradition of the Stage Manager assuming this role is still very much alive.

Performance

The largest and probably most obvious area in which a Stage Manager is going to be maintaining show is in the cast performance. One of the truly exciting things about live theatre versus film or TV, is the constantly evolving development of characters. In film, a character is only developed as far as the final take is set, at which point the Director assembles a performance in the editing room and it is locked forever. In the theatre, over the course of rehearsals and performance, actors are going to naturally discover new and interesting things about the character, and that's going to alter their approach to performing each night. During rehearsals, a consensus will hopefully have been reached between the actors and the Director about what the show as a whole, and specific scenes, are trying to say. The element that is missing from those rehearsals, however, is the audience. How an audience receives the production can greatly inform an actor's performance, which is why most shows have a preview period. The preview period is designed to allow the creative team and the cast to adapt the show based on the audience's response before opening night. However, that discovery process does not stop at opening, so the trick for the Stage Manager is to differentiate between natural growth and altering the intention as they try to maintain the show.

Natural growth is going to be characterized by slight adjustments to tempo or intonation without significantly changing the meaning or pacing of the show. The Stage Manager must monitor the show from both a micro and macro perspective as they determine the impact of these incremental shifts on the production overall. For example, in the case of comedic shows the audience has a definitive impact on the pacing of the production through laughter. The cast will have spent weeks in rehearsal with only the other people in the room to play off of, but once they get into performance there are hundreds or thousands of people that they are playing to. Let's say that a given scene is written to be very fast paced, and that speed is what drives the comedy. In the midst of the scene is a gag that elicited three seconds of laughter in rehearsal, but the cast was directed to move on from it after that point to keep the scene moving forward. In performance, that gag may now garner seven to ten seconds of laughter. That is a significantly longer pause that they now need to take in order to adapt to it. Sometimes, that joke stops being funny for the actor so they make a slight adjustment to the way they perform the gag to keep it fresh for themselves. It still gets the laugh and the actor feels better about not just repeating the same thing every day. Other times that little adjustment will garner an even bigger laugh and that seven to ten seconds skews closer to thirteen. Now that gag becomes a bit of a game. That little adjustment clearly was a better choice than what had been done in rehearsal, so the actor keeps the adjustment and then takes it a little bit further. Now they start to extend their pause in order to draw out the laugh as long as possible and it starts to hit the seventeen- to twenty-second mark. That long pause has now totally derailed the pacing of the rest of that scene. The Stage Manager must now make a decision about how to intervene in the situation.

1 **Assess the impact**

   The first step in dealing with maintaining the cast's performance is to assess the impact of the changes that are occurring. This impact is not solely restricted to the audience's experience but the other cast members as well. Are the changes altering the intention of the Director, as you understand it? Are the changes adding time to the show? Are the changes forcing other cast members to alter their performance to compensate? All of these are valid and important questions to ask as you determine whether the adjustments are detrimental to the performance.

2 **Determine the immediacy**

   Part of the assessment process may be to let the changes ride for a couple of performances to see if they clear up themselves. Often an actor will try something new and determine that it does not work on their own. They too are watching out for the good of the production, in the same way that the Stage Manager does, so giving them the benefit of the doubt is often useful and appropriate. However, there are times when deviations are egregious enough that they need to be addressed immediately. It is up to the Stage Manager to determine the immediacy of the response and that immediacy is usually linked directly to the impact on the production. Any adjustments that would impact the safety of anyone in the cast need to be dealt with immediately. This can even mean addressing it as soon as the cast member comes offstage or even holding a performance if the situation is dangerous enough. Company morale is also important to consider when determining the immediacy of giving performance notes. If someone has been having a difficult time personally, if it is the end of the week and people are exhausted, or even if you have just given notes recently it may be worthwhile to give it a few days before going in with another round.

3   Reading the room

As has been discussed several times, reading the room is critical in any communication the Stage Manager does. The nature of the job requires the Stage Manager to work with many different personality types, so maintaining an awareness of how people respond to notes in general and divining the best moments that they will be most receptive is a skill that all Stage Managers must develop. There are certainly those who give notes almost robotically and feel that absolutely every change should be addressed immediately. This method can often lead to frustration among the cast as it appears the Stage Manager is not sensitive to the work they are doing. That sensitivity is key and is why taking the time to assess the impact of these deviations, and determining how immediate the response needs to be, is important.

Giving notes to the cast after opening is always a delicate process and this is one of the reasons that building a strong foundation of trust with the cast is critical throughout the rehearsal process. Once the Director is gone the cast needs to be able to trust both the objective and subjective artistic opinions of the Stage Manager when they are trying to give notes. As much as the Stage Manager is trying to maintain the Director's intention, they are also serving as the eyes and ears of the cast, and need to be a resource to them in moments of insecurity, or just curiosity. Experiencing the audience as you perform is very different from being an objective observer of the performance. Everyone is naturally their own worst critic and so it is not uncommon for cast members to ask the Stage Manager for their opinion of their performance on any given night. If they don't trust the Stage Manager's opinion then the Stage Manager loses the ability to be a support system for the cast in that way. Losing that is quite problematic as this is a fundamental part of the actor–SM relationship.

This part of the relationship is also the bridge into being able to give notes effectively throughout the run. The reality is that the cast has likely not seen the Stage Manager as an artistic force in the process up until the show opens. There is always the exception of those unique shows where the Director leans on the Stage Manager artistically but, by and large, it is common for the cast members to not get a sense of the Stage Manager as an artist until the show opens. There are two main approaches to giving notes to the cast as a Stage Manager:

1 **The logistical approach**

Some Stage Managers see their role in the maintenance of a show as simply reminding the cast of the things they "should" be doing, based on the Director's notes throughout the process. And, truth be told, that is what the Stage Manager is meant to do. However, thinking of it this way often leads to a very cold approach to fulfilling that role. For Stage Managers who do not see themselves as artists, or are not willing to assume the role of an artist in show maintenance, giving notes to the cast becomes like giving notes about prop placement to the crew. They pull out their carefully archived paperwork about staging and look at the timings, and use concrete and quantifiable data as their way to get the show back on track. They steer clear of meaning or intention and focus squarely on ensuring that people are standing where they are supposed to be standing and that the show is clocking in at the time it is supposed to. By removing themselves from any artistic conversation, they absolve themselves from any disputes that may arise regarding the approach to the show. This approach is only going to work to a point, however. What happens when a cast member comes to the Stage Manager with a complaint about the way another cast member's altered performance is effecting their own? In that scenario, it is not possible for the Stage Manager to stick solely to blocking notation and timings as their only way to discuss getting the show back to where it is supposed to be. In those situations, the Stage Manager can try to mediate the conversation between the two cast members or try to throw the issue to the producers, but being willing and able to use an artistic vocabulary to have that conversation would make dealing with the issue much easier.

2 The artistic approach

As with any communication, the most effective way to get your point across and have a conversation is to speak the same language. This approach to giving notes is rooted in that notion. While the responsibility of the Stage Manager to maintain the artistic integrity of the show that the Director and creative team mounted remains consistent, the Stage Manager takes greater artistic ownership of the show after opening. Whether they agree with the creative choices that have been made or not, they take note of the Director's thought process during the rehearsal process, and not just the nuts and bolts of the blocking. In this way, they are able to better ensure that the production remains aligned with the Director's original intention. It also means that when giving notes to the cast, they are able to communicate in language that feels familiar and consistent with what they have heard up until this point. By taking a more artist-based approach to the notes, the Stage Manager is able to relate to the cast's onstage experience a bit more than the nuts and bolts version. They are able to communicate motivations and provide creative solutions to bring the show back to the originally intended vision. In the case of the actor whose performance is being negatively impacted by another actor's changes, the Stage Manager will have a much easier time discussing the issue with both performers. The Stage Manager has a much larger array of tools to pull from as they talk about what has shifted in their respective performances and how one has impacted the other, always with the goal of finding a middle ground that works for all parties. Being willing to converse about someone's artistry in the same terms that they do builds a more collaborative environment and makes the performer more receptive to the Stage Manager's thoughts. By removing the art from the conversation you are cutting off a valuable avenue of communication.

It is important to remember that as the show grows naturally it cannot remain exactly the same as it was on opening night. Part of the joy of live theatre is that constant evolution, so the key for the Stage Manager is to have a clear understanding of the original intent of the direction and to have the vocabulary to work with the cast to ensure the production doesn't stray far from that intent.

Safety calls and brush-ups

As a part of the maintenance aspect of the Stage Manager's job after opening is the overseeing of various types of safety calls and brush-up rehearsals. Any show that includes action that can be deemed dangerous should have a separate call to rehearse that action prior to each performance. These calls are designed to keep people safe and ensure that they are not walking on stage cold to do something that could hurt themselves or others. The two most common safety calls are *fight calls* and *dance calls*.

Fight calls

Fight calls are instituted any time a show includes fight choreography. Whether an onstage fight is hyperrealistic or highly stylized, a fight call is an important part of making sure everyone onstage is safe each night. Every bit of fight choreography needs to be worked during a fight call so the time allotted to it will vary show to show. Sometimes it is just a single slap and you only need a few minutes, but on a show such as *Romeo and Juliet* a fight call could last thirty to forty-five minutes, or longer. Almost every fight call is structured in the same way.

1   The cast members involved go through the entire fight at 25 percent of full speed. This allows the cast members to remember what they are supposed to be doing, just in case they have forgotten something. Even though they may have been doing the same fight over and over for weeks, there is always to the chance that someone's mind will go blank. Slowly stepping through the fight bit by bit ensures that everyone has the fight in their bodies.

2   Next, they will do the fight again, this time at 50 percent. By doing the fight again, a bit faster, they can start to work up to performance speed. The initial run at 25 percent can also feel quite awkward so moving to 50 percent shakes off some of that weirdness and gets them ready for full speed.

3   There are a couple of schools of thought on the final run of the fight. Some believe the cast should go through it at 75 percent speed. By never getting to show speed they cannot get overly comfortable, which is when accidents happen. It also leaves a little room for performance energy to kick in. The other way would be to go to show speed. There is benefit to doing that so that the cast can say they have done it at

the speed it will be performed but, again, performance energy will naturally push people to go a little harder. By not bumping up against the performance ceiling the cast will have somewhere to go.

At the end of the day, the way in which fight calls are run is up to the fight captain on a show. While the Stage Manager maintains ultimate responsibility for the safety of the cast, the fight captain is specifically responsible for the fight choreography. They are usually assigned to the post by the fight choreographer and tend to be the most knowledgeable about stage fighting in the cast. They must learn the choreography and will normally watch the fights from the side lines to ensure everyone is being safe. If they have to participate in the fights they will often ask the Stage Manager to be an extra set of eyes and will break up the fight calls to be able to watch the elements in which they are not involved in isolation before joining in themselves.

Dance calls

Structured in a very similar way to fight calls are *dance calls*. Now the term dance calls is very generic and it is rare that it is used in practice on a show. Normally these are broken down into the type of movement that is being rehearsed; for example, *lift call, tumbling call*, etc. The umbrella term of dance calls encompasses any type of choreography, outside of fights, that could be deemed dangerous and need to be rehearsed. The most common of these is lifts. Any specialized lift in a show should be rehearsed preshow. This is especially true of moments when nondancers are being lifted. It is ultimately up to the dance captain and performers to determine which general dancer lifts should be rehearsed as a part of the lift call, but the Stage Manager needs to insist that any lifts of a principal cast member be addressed. There are always going to be exceptions to the rule, but the overall principal should be to touch upon them before each performance.

More and more, musical theatre is adding acrobatics and gymnastics to the bench of available skills to be used in choreography. These stunts include back flips, somersaults, high jumps, front flips, etc. All of these should be rehearsed before the show. No matter how proficient a performer may be, giving them the opportunity to go through the moves in isolation provides everyone with peace of mind. That being said, it is important to remember that the performer is the expert on these moves and their own bodies, so you must remain sensitive to the fact that they may need to handle these calls in a different way than you might want them to. As long as they are being safe and getting what they need out of the safety call it is okay to support their preference, but know that these, more than fight calls, are a negotiation with the performer. They are for them, after all.

Company morale

Depending on the length of the run of the show, a single group of people can be working together, in close quarters, for weeks, months, or even years. Each day they go through the same routine, interacting with the same people, and it can get trying after a while. While it is not an explicit part of the Stage Manager's job to organize events or bring in treats, there is a great benefit to trying to keep the morale of the cast and crew as high as possible throughout a run. Various people on a production may take ownership of this task, but it is important for the Stage Manager to be monitoring the overall morale as it can have a dramatic impact on the quality of the performance and working environment of everyone on the show. In union settings, the Stage Manager is going to be the first person to which the cast's union representative is going to come to discuss discontent in the workplace, and it frankly behooves the Stage Manager to try to deter any unhappiness for the company's own sake. A happy company is also a company that is going to be more receptive to performance notes, schedule changes, added rehearsals, and any number of other things that might otherwise upset people.

One of the best ways to keep company morale high is by building a sense of community from the outset. The cast is going to be working closely in a rehearsal room for weeks before moving to the theater, so they will have already built some kind of dynamic. That dynamic, however, is built based on a very active working environment where everyone is trying to get up to speed on the production. They are learning new things and pushing themselves to be ready for performance, which can be very stressful. That stress can bond people very deeply, but once the stress of preparation is removed, a new status quo needs to be established. All of a sudden people are not spending eight hours a day in a rehearsal room together. They are coming in half an hour to an hour prior to curtain and going to their dressing rooms to get ready. There aren't lunch breaks for them to spend time together so, unless they are sharing a dressing room, people often disperse once a run starts. Once the cast moves into the theater there is a dynamic shift as the crew is integrated. These two groups are learning to work together and, often, the crew works for the venue and already has their own relationships. The cast can feel like visitors in someone else's house, so trying to build a bridge between the two from the outset is going to benefit everyone. The reality, however, is that there may not be time to do a lot of team bonding during tech so once the show opens this may be the first opportunity to really bring everyone together.

Morale-boosting activities

1 **The backdeck BBQ**

One of the most common team building and morale boosting activities in the theatre is the BBQ. For some theatre companies and venues this is a tradition that goes back many years. Backdeck BBQs are usually hosted by the crew in the loading dock of the theater. Someone will bring in or purchase a venue specific grill and everyone will bring something to cook up. These are usually held on weekends, in between matinee and evening performances, and can be a great way to get people together to have some fun and celebrate the end of a hard week. Places such as the Kirk Douglas Theatre in Culver City, CA, host a BBQ every Sunday in between shows. Everyone working that day is invited, and this way not just the crew and cast, but also the ushers and administrative staff are brought into the fold and get to spend some time together. Holding them weekly also takes some of the pressure off. If you want to meet a friend for lunch or run errands between shows, you are not missing a specifically planned special event because you can always come next week. Other companies, such as Cincinnati Opera, host a massive BBQ for the season. In this case everyone working on a show in their summer season is invited, and it serves as a kickoff to the summer and a chance for everyone to get to meet, even if they won't necessarily be working together that season. However you choose to do it, these BBQs are a very easy way to get people talking and hopefully build some positive relationships that will carry the show through closing.

2 **Birthdays and other occasions**

Another great way to show people that they are appreciated is by acknowledging special occasions in their lives. The easiest of these is birthdays, but anniversaries, births of children, marriages, and other milestones are all worth acknowledging and can bring people together in a more personal way. Of course, sometimes shows are not running long enough for everyone to have a birthday or other major life events happen, but no matter what, acknowledging the ones that do come along is an important part of building a community among the company. Acknowledging these life events can be as easy as having everyone sign a card for the individual, but more commonly someone will bring in a cake or some kind of treat.

3 **Random treats**

One of the best ways to improve morale is to bring in treats without any advance warning. If it seems like people are dragging or feeling sluggish, bringing in cookies or cupcakes (or anything really) can help to give everyone a boost. Unexpected acknowledgement of everyone's good work is a great way to make them feel a bit better. Doing the same thing day in and day out can be draining and it is easy to feel like your work has become unappreciated, so having a surprise thank-you can do a lot to bolster people's spirits.

4 **Postshow drinks**

First of all, this is not meant to advocate drinking, but the reality is that getting a drink with your coworkers is a very traditional way to bond. It is also a mainstay of theatre culture. Because people who work in the theatre start and end work late, going out for dinner is not usually an option and lunch requires people to come in early. The easy alternative to these is to go to a bar following a performance and have a drink and small bite to eat. The tone of this activity can vary greatly depending on the people you are with, so be careful about your expectations of this. Sometimes postshow drinks can be very tame and sometimes quite raucous, so being aware of where you are going and who you are going with is important, but it is a great way to get to know people outside of work in a more causal, social setting.

These are just a few of the most common group morale activities, but be creative about how you try to keep morale up. With smaller groups, family dinners are always a lovely way to make people feel included and keep a team bonded. Many stage management teams will do this before a show. They come in early and all get dinner together. It gives the team the opportunity to hang out and enjoy each other, and helps to lessen the divide that tends to occur once a show opens. At the end of the day, any activity that brings people together and acknowledges their contribution to the show is going to go a long way toward creating a positive working environment. The more content and happy people are the less likely they are to want to leave, and the more pleasant the workplace will feel.

After opening, the Stage Manager takes on a whole new role. Depending on the individual, this can be a new and exciting challenge, or a frustrating and laborious addition to the workload. Either way, absorbing the role of caretaker for a production positions the Stage Manager to engage with the cast and crew in a way they may not have up until that point. It also underlines the need for the Stage Manager to be clued in to every part of the creative and technical process as a show is mounted. Everyone has their own interests and strengths, of course, but it is important that the Stage Manager takes the time to fully understand the approach and intent of each member of the creative team. If they don't, how will they be able to confidently maintain the production past opening?

It can be easy to fall into the trap of only focusing on the things that are pertinent in the moment as you go through a rehearsal, but looking at the long game is what will make you successful in the end. The job of the Stage Manager is incredibly busy, from beginning to end, but it is made easier the more you pay attention. The more information and understanding that the Stage Manager has, the easier it becomes to anticipate what is coming and put out those fires in advance. It also makes the process of keeping the show clean, tight, and functioning well during the run that much smoother. Many people find themselves moving into stage management because it allows them the opportunity to be involved in every element of the process. The actual run of the show is the payoff of all of that involvement. Whether it is overall show maintenance or keeping up the team's morale, the more interest the Stage Manager shows, and the more information they retain, the more positive a show experience will be for them and everyone around them.

6

Working with Others

One of the most compelling and exciting elements about working in the arts is the incredible diversity it attracts. Diversity of peoples, cultures, ideas, mediums, styles, structures, and any other kind imaginable. Throughout history, the arts at large (not just the performing arts) have created a platform for artists to express themselves and their ideas with the only limit being their own creativity. This culture of collaborative expression has a negative side as well. In bringing together a broad group of people with varying viewpoints and approaches, the door is instantly opened to conflict around any number of issues.

The Stage Manager has the unique opportunity to engage with absolutely everyone involved in a production. Almost everyone else on the production team is boxed in to working with the people most closely associated with their area. The Stage Manager, however, is required to find a way to work efficiently and collegially with everyone, even if they don't necessarily get along with them. Beyond having to develop a functional working relationship with everyone, by virtue of their position they will also likely find themselves in the middle of phenomenal collaborations and massive falling-outs among those that they are working with. Being capable of effectively mediating any disputes that arise is a critical skill that all Stage Managers must possess.

Teamwork and collaboration

Industry-wide, it is common to refer to the collection of Stage Managers on a project as the "stage management team." The word "team" is key as these individuals must develop a relationship that will allow them to trust and rely on each other to be able to make a show happen. Without a positive culture of collaboration and open communication among the Stage Managers the team will fracture and the likelihood of errors and dangerous mistakes increases.

Most shows have many moving and overlapping components and it is critical that the Stage Managers are working together to ensure that nothing gets missed. Often people who go into stage management are "Type A"-driven, and tend to want to be in control of every situation. This can often lead to believing that in order to get something right they must do it themselves. It is fine, and important, for Stage Managers to take ownership of their work, but it is critical to remember that they do not work in a vacuum. There are other members of the team to provide insight, expertise, and support, and making use of those resources is what will make for a more fulfilling professional experience. Simply by the nature of the way theatre works, there is going be a massive amount of information coming to the Stage Managers throughout the production process.

As with any team, the Stage Managers involved in a show are all going to have different strengths and styles, and finding a comfortable way to meld those is important. From time to time disagreements will arise that will potentially cause problems and hamper the team's ability to work cohesively, but as the primary support structure for any show the stage management team needs to be able to work through those issues.

Despite whatever differences they may have, Stage Managers have a very unique position within live entertainment and can provide a level of understanding for each other that no one else can. These team members will certainly be coworkers but in many cases they can often become the best of friends, or even start to feel like family. Many companies work with the same Stage Managers regularly, and so the same faces will cycle through a theater over and over again. This consistency in staffing patterns supports a closer team dynamic but can also breed competition and disagreements. Maintaining high morale among the team is important in combatting potential issues down the road.

Opera companies are a prime example. Opera companies often have shows running simultaneously in order to maintain a full week of performances on their schedule. As will be discussed in the opera chapter (Chapter 7), most operas only perform once or twice a week in order to allow singers to rest their voices and so, if multiple shows are running in repertory, there will be multiple stage management teams sharing the building, sharing office space, or even sharing a desk. In this environment, the Stage Managers are working in close proximity, even if they are not working on the same show. Often, there is a culture of mutual support that is developed between the different teams because other Stage Managers are the only ones who fully understand what each other are going through. When one team is in tech, the other may bring in treats or organize a "family" dinner to get everyone together. Using colleagues to create a strong support structure can make all the difference in career longevity.

In talking to Stage Managers who have gone on to work in more traditional office settings, one of the first things they identify as being something they miss from their freelance days is the camaraderie and support that their teammates provide. There is an intimacy in those relationship because you are working together to accomplish a very specific goal. Stage Managers are sharing a singular experience. They have similar backgrounds and similar job responsibilities, and they are working on a specific show together. Don't take that for granted. Whether or not everyone has different styles and don't always agree, it's important to at least acknowledge that they understand what you're going through and are hopefully rooting for you to succeed.

Conflict in the room

At the beginning of every rehearsal process the Stage Manager walks into a room with a group of new people with diverse personalities, and while that is incredibly exciting it also comes with the realization that it may already be too late to head off potential conflicts among those individuals. This is not meant to sound dour or pessimistic, but the reality is that the Stage Manager, like everyone else, needs to learn who these people are and discover what the dynamic on this particular project is before beginning to head-off potential problems. Accepting the fact that management of the personalities on a show is an on-the-fly art is the first step to successfully building a positive working environment and relationship with your colleagues. You need to be ready to be flexible and to try to convince others to be as well.

Many Stage Managers will find themselves put in situations where something feels above their pay grade, or that they are unqualified to be able to respond to a specific question or concern that is being voiced by an actor, director, or any other creative team member. Often, the best thing they can do in these situations is to just manage the personalities, rather than the situation. It's more about keeping the people they are around calm and trying to get to whatever the root issue is, so that the appropriate person can manage the conflict in an informed way. Because the Stage Manager is always in the rehearsal room, it is almost certain that they will be the face of management that is present when conflict arises. It cannot be reiterated enough how critical it is to remember that the Stage Manager does not work in a vacuum. There is almost always going to be someone in a higher-level position who will get involved in serious conflicts. Involving Producers, Production Managers, and others is not only better for the Stage Manager's personal mental health, it is better for the show that the Stage Manager remains a positive and neutral force whose priority is the well-being of the show. Identifying when to personally step in to solve a problem and when to involve others comes with experience.

Stories from the front lines

Let's say, for example, that you're working with a team of people who have never collaborated with each other before. Your job, as the Stage Manager, is to try and make sure that the rehearsal process goes along as smoothly as possible and that you're supporting the process of the creative team so that they feel like they can do what they need to do. All of a sudden communication starts to break down between the creative team members. It's not your fault, but it is now your problem.

A recent production was produced with a director and a designer who had never worked together before. They were both incredibly enthusiastic about collaborating on this very ambitious project. All their initial meetings went beautifully. Following extensive conversation and hours of meetings they walked away with what they thought was a clear and mutual understanding of the next steps that needed to be to be taken. Unfortunately, the reality was that they had very different perspectives on what had actually been agreed to. When they did come back together the Director felt like the designer had not delivered on what they had planned; meanwhile the designer felt that they had fulfilled all of their obligations. Neither party was willing to back down on what they believed had been agreed upon before they went away and so they were at an impasse. With neither person budging, and a limited rehearsal schedule, the Stage Manager, Production Manager, and Producer had to mediate the disagreement and try to help to find a way forward.

In this case, the situation devolved very quickly. Tempers and frustrations were high and the parties involved had very strong opinions about who was right and wrong. When there is little-to-no room for compromise, mediating the situation can become almost impossible. In this case, the best that the mediators could do was to calm tempers enough for the creative team to push through the next few days of a brief rehearsal process.

For the Stage Manager, inserting themselves into a situation like this is going to be a delicate proposition. Ultimately, the disagreement is happening between these two people and it's not really the job of the Stage Manager to try and fix their personal relationship, but a compromise needs to be reached to keep the project moving forward. So how does a Stage Manager mediate that discussion? How do they get these two people to adapt to the current circumstances, despite frustrations and hard feelings?

1. Keep it private

First of all, the situation needs to be addressed privately. Often these kinds of confrontations occur in full view of the cast, crew, and other creative team members. Allowing the argument to happen in full public view is not professionally acceptable, nor helpful to anyone on the team. Pull the conflicting powers out of the rehearsal room and out of earshot of the cast. Giving people in conflict an audience often leads to greater power struggles and will escalate the confrontation, as the parties will be less likely to compromise and risk being seen as weak. Allowing them to display this behavior can also have a detrimental effect on their relationship with the group moving forward. Watching a nasty fight unfold will invariably color the cast's view of those involved.

2. Start a dialogue

Much of the time, conflicts within a production develop due to a miscommunication. One person expected one thing and the other expected something else and now they are insistent on getting what they wanted in the beginning. These unmet expectations can lead to individuals digging their heels in and a total unwillingness to compromise. Obviously, collaboration and compromise go hand in hand and it is important to remind people of that. When a conflict initially arises, often the individuals will simply repeat or restate their desire or perspective over and over again. It can become a situation where they are trapped in a loop where neither is listening to the other and so no progress can be made. Pushing them to start a dialogue is the best way to get them back to collaborating.

A great technique to use to achieve dialogue is for the mediator to step in to restate the problem and present a very general solution. Again, creative team disputes are not necessarily the Stage Manager's to completely solve but they can help mediate the discussion. When people get locked in during a confrontation of this nature, they often cannot see another solution to the problem other than the one they themselves have come up with. The mediator, as an objective party, can help getting them talking by being the outside voice trying to marry the two dueling opinions. It does not mean that the option they come up with will be the one that is utilized, but it will at least break the cycle of fighting over a single idea. It also will provide a new topic of discussion that will hopefully get the two people in conflict to focus on debating another concept that neither is strongly invested in. This can help to spur new ideas as they are not trying to win any longer.

3. Establishing next steps

Once those in conflict are in a dialogue and some headway starts being made, establishing a path forward is critical. What are the next steps? What needs to be achieved in order for the rehearsal to continue to be productive? At some point the fact that one did not understand the other becomes irrelevant and it becomes more important to identify how we move forward. It can be difficult to get people to realize that point; to give up their fundamental argumentative position and start to realize: "Okay this is where we are so how do we progress?"

Creating a bullet-point task list for each person can help to clarify what decisions have been made and ensure that everyone is on the same page. As this list is created ask the following questions:

1   What was the root cause of the conflict? Identifying if this is an isolated incident or a systemic problem due to contrasting personalities will help you to target how to lay out the structure of how to move forward.

2   What does each party need in order to do their job? Get very specific about the needs of each person. In resolving the conflict, being too

vague can only open the door to more issues. Take the time to talk out what the itemized plan for progressing is. This will not only help to assure you haven't missed anything while talking through the plan, but will also force the individuals to hear things from the other person's perspective.

3 What is the timeline for completion? Get specific about when results need to be seen and help to negotiate what that timeline is. As the master of the show's schedule, the Stage Manager can help to provide the broad-view perspective of how one deadline will affect another.

Laying all of this out verbally, or on paper, will help everyone in the process of moving forward. It is also wise to write it all out and send it along to the Producers or Production Manager when it's all complete. They will need to be looped into whatever happened anyways, and providing them with a clear picture on where things landed will better help their ability to support you and everyone on the project in the future.

Problems from within

Most of what has been discussed revolves around conflicts between creative team or cast members, but what happens when one of these difficult personalities is on the stage management team? What happens when there is an ASM who is not responding well to working in the way that the show requires? What happens when the Stage Manager is not living up to the obligations of their position? Dealing with conflict occurring within their own team can be one of the most difficult situations a Stage Manager has to deal with.

The Stage Manager is charged with overseeing the management of a complete production and being situated in that position allows them to set the tone and work style they would like their stage management team to follow. Stage Managers tend to possess some natural leadership abilities and that helps them to manage their staff. One of the potential difficulties, however, is that their staff is comprised of other Type A leaders. If the Stage Manager has been able to put together a cohesive team they will hopefully be receptive to the SM's leadership and be respectful of the various styles that their colleagues bring to the work. Ninety-five percent of the time it all works beautifully and the Stage Managers on a project work very well together. Even if there is disagreement, everyone is still able to find a path to collaboration without ever having to have a serious conversation about how to get along. The other 5 percent of the time issues arise. How those issues are handled will make all the difference in the success of the team moving forward.

1 If someone is working in a way that you do not agree with, make sure you understand the other person's reasons. If you are the Stage Manager, do not just simply assume that one of your ASMs has gone rogue because they're not doing things the way you personally would. Don't immediately dismiss the style or approach your ASM may have, because it may be completely valid for both the situation and the person. Methods of conflict resolution are not one-size-fits-all.

2 Be open to learning from those you work with. Do not fall into the trap of thinking that you know everything or think you need to be perceived as doing everything. Ignoring someone else's contributions and assuming that you are the only one that knows the right way can be detrimental to the project, not to mention the damage it can do to the personal relationship you're trying to develop with your team. Part of the Stage Manager's job is to get people onboard with an approach to handling a project. They can't successfully do that if they feel that their own experience and knowledge is being dismissed. They may work with you, but it will be begrudgingly. Get to know the ASMs and the crew, and trust and rely on their expertise. Micromanage only when absolutely necessary. One of the best signs of a good ASM is when the Stage Manager does not need to know what they are doing. As long as the work is getting done, and getting done well, the team is working. Trust in people's ability to handle things as they see fit.

3 Assess whether the approach that they are using works. How detrimental is it to the production that they are doing things their way rather than yours? Make sure you're checking in with yourself, make sure your discontent with their approach is not rooted in your ego. If you are planning to call someone on your team out on their work you should be confident that your reasons are justified.

Being selective in the choice of battles to engage in is important when working closely with someone for any length of time. If the determination is made that the situation needs to be addressed, approach the conversation respectfully. Be as assertive as is necessary but avoid inflammatory language and do not allow it to feel like a personal attack. Remember that the Stage Manager is running a team, so framing the conversation to better improve the team dynamic is one of the best ways to set the right tone. The goal here should be to guide the stage management staff to make positive changes in the way they are working, and not to dictate they must do it a certain way. Allow this to be a true conversation. There are of course going to be situations where people will be obstinate and the SM will have to dictate, but that should not be their first move.

Throwing a cliché out there, leading by example is the best way to get people onboard with your style. Before sitting down and having a conversation about someone else's behavior or someone else's professional choices, make sure that your past actions have been reasonable and ones you can be proud of. Your own behavior, not position, is what will give you credibility and that is the example that you're going to need to present. Should the other party get defensive, it is also the example that's going to get thrown back at you. Again, self-assessment is critical to success in any leadership role. There is a difference between being the boss and leading a team. Leaders take the time to evaluate their behavior, whereas bosses issue directives without regard for hypocrisy. Evaluate your choices and make sure, not that you've never made a mistake but, that you recognize where your strengths and where your flaws are. Be willing to identify and discuss them. Owning the things that you have done wrong will help people to become less combative. It will also help you to recognize the other person's contributions; for example, "I don't understand automation at all, which is why it is so great that you are on the show, since you have so much experience with it." Acknowledging that the other person has unique expertise makes them feel more valued and will make them more receptive to constructive criticism, or instruction, on their weaknesses.

People, by nature, are defensive. They do not like to be told they are wrong, and so they may push back. Being open, honest, and nonegotistical is one of the best ways to try and keep people from getting too defensive and from losing sight of the fact that you are in this together. It can also be very helpful to take some of those negative examples about yourself and use those to help identify what the other person is doing that's problematic to the process. Using examples of personal failings to help frame how the other person can improve helps to lower their defensiveness because they feel less attacked and more like they are being looked out for.

Putting it into practice

Let's say that you're in the rehearsal room as the production Stage Manager and your ASM has been regularly walking in and out of the door, making a ruckus and distracting from the process. You have started to realize that it's frustrating not only to you but also to the Director. The Director hasn't said anything to you yet, but you can see the look on their face every time this person decides that it's necessary to go in and out. And so it seems to be reaching a point where someone has to say something and, as it is your staff, it is your responsibility to handle it. First you pull them aside privately:

PSM Look I've noticed that you've been going in and out a lot and it's causing a bit of a distraction.

ASM I am doing my job. I need to be grabbing props from the hallway and how else am I supposed to do it?

PSM I totally get it. I am just wondering if there is anything we can do to limit the distraction. Would it be helpful if I gave you a hand organizing the props that we need for the whole day right at the beginning? That way you will only have to go in and out when we add something?

ASM That might help.

PSM Great! I am happy to do that. I think it will also help us in the long run with just the visual of our preparedness.

ASM What do you mean?

PSM Well, like, I used to always run around trying to get things done but I kept getting the note that I appeared to be out of control. I didn't feel at all like I was out of control but to everyone else it seemed like I was super stressed out.

ASM Oh gotcha. Have you heard that about me?

PSM No. Not at all, but I think the more stable we appear in the room the better it will be for us in the long run. If you only have to scramble for something brand new it will just help to instill that much more confidence.

I don't intend that exchange to sound too movie-of-the-week but I think it provides a nice jumping-off point for conversation. The PSM is able to address the primary concern (the ASM is becoming distracted by running in and out of the rehearsal room) in a constructive and supportive way. The ASM is receptive to the note and gladly accepts the PSM's assistance. The PSM is also able to call out another, secondary (but critical) issue of the optics of having someone running in and out. They were able to kill two birds with one stone and accomplish it without ruffling feathers but still being able to address the problems clearly and directly.

Obviously, this exchange was an idyllic one but also not entirely unrealistic. I can honestly say that the vast majority of conversations of this type that I have had to have played out in a very similar fashion. Should the conversation devolve and become combative you will have to use your instincts to figure out how to move it forward but try to keep some of these concepts in mind. The more you can place the focus on respect, team building, and protecting the production, the easier it will be to maintain a positive relationship with your colleagues.

The next obvious question is: "What happens when an ASM is working with a Stage Manager who is struggling to live up to the responsibilities of their job?" Are they allowed to say something? Is it appropriate? Is it acceptable? And if they do decide to say something will they ever work again? These are all completely reasonable questions to ask. Calling out a supervisor for bad behavior, or not doing their job properly, is a dangerous prospect in any profession. Due to the collaborative nature of the theatre, however, there are ways to help improve a less-than-desirable situation.

1   Identify that there is a problem. Very similar to the initial steps a Stage Manager would take in assessing internal team issues, make sure that this is not just being personally bothered by something that nobody else seems to have a problem with. Again, it is important to pick your fights so be sure that any action taken is not unwarranted. Just as the Stage Manager manages a team of Type A, leader-oriented people, the ASM is being managed by one. One of the most common points of conflict within a stage management team is an ASM who has difficulty being led. Because people in this profession tend to move fluidly between taking the Stage Manager role and the ASM role, some people struggle with going from being in charge to having to follow someone else's lead. This can sometimes color their perspective as they observe

the Stage Manager's work. This is why serious personal evaluation is necessary to ensure a perceived problem actually needs addressing.

2 In every relationship and every professional setting there is a line that should not be crossed. Where that line exists is going to differ depending on the people you're working with and the institution that you're working for. Many companies hire the same Stage Managers over and over again. Sometimes this is because the Stage Manager is so good they deserve it, but often this rehiring has to do with loyalty. Companies will overlook problematic aspects of Stage Managers because there's a comfort level associated with their presence, as "they know the company." It often feels safer to hire someone known to be flawed, rather than taking a risk on hiring someone brand new. This can also be true for some directors. A director may have a favorite Stage Manager who they've been working with for decades and they will continue to work with because that person makes them feel comfortable. Understanding the relationship between the Stage Manager and the Director/institution can help you figure out how to navigate any differences you may have. This relationship will also help to determine how worthwhile what will ultimately be an awkward conversation would be.

3 Finally, weigh the benefit of the actions planned against the potential fallout. You have to go forward working alongside the Stage Manager and with any tension that may arise after the issue is discussed. This working relationship will exist, not only for the length of a production but indefinitely. As a freelancer, it is important to protect your reputation and to temper frustration against how taking action might impact job prospects. Obviously, if there is a question of safety there should be no hesitation, but if the concern is more about personal taste, be sure to take the time to consider the ramifications. Part of this is understanding the personality of the Stage Manager you are working with. Gauge what their reaction might be before going down a confrontational path.

Stories from the front lines

At the end of the day, just like the Stage Manager, the ASM is looking out for the welfare of the show. While the ASM should not undermine or side-step the Stage Manager, there are ways to walk a line where you actively support them and try to smooth out some of the metaphorical wrinkles.

There was a particular instance where an ASM worked with a Stage Manager who had been around a long time and, in many ways, lost their passion for the job. They seemed to very much enjoy the position but not necessarily the duties involved. Schedules would be incorrect, information provided to creative teams would be wrong, breaks would be forgotten, and communication would be inefficient and unclear. The Stage Manager had a long-standing relationship with both the Producers and the Director and so no one was willing to say anything to him. Initially the ASM was very reticent to do anything. He tried to stick to his job responsibilities alone and stay focused on doing his part well.

After about a week it became clear that the Stage Manager's approach was beginning to have a detrimental impact on the show. The Director was becoming progressively more frustrated and the cast was losing their patience. The ASM knew that he was in no position to call him out and so he decided to start filling in gaps. Rather than sitting quietly, he started offering suggestions and volunteering to assist whenever he saw something about to get forgotten. He provided correct information and became the primary resource for the Technical Director. This added a certain burden to his shoulders but was in the best interest of the production. Taking on the extra responsibility was good for both the production and for the ASM professionally, so he was more than willing.

During this entire process, the ASM walked a very delicate line of trying not to undermine the Stage Manager. He did not want to alienate him, nor be perceived as trying to take over. This was true in the rehearsal room but became of paramount importance when they moved into the theater. The ASM did not want to detract from the Stage Manager's credibility with the crew. They needed to be able to draw their own conclusion, uncolored by the ASM's feelings. It was also important that he not come across as an overly ambitious ASM who was trying to take over the show. Instilling that perception in the crew was not in his best interest either. The situation eventually resolved itself following that production when the Stage Manager retired and the ASM was hired as the SM in subsequent productions with the same producer. This all may sound like a very passive approach to dealing with the situation but these types of scenarios need to be handled very delicately.

The good stuff

Most of this chapter has been about various types of conflict resolution and dealing with difficult people, but what about the positive side of the working relationships built as a Stage Manager? At the end of the day, the key to success in the entertainment industry is who you know. Building strong relationships with a diverse group of people in every discipline is what will keep a Stage Manager working for the length of their career. For better or for worse, your reputation will always precede you, so passionately protecting that is of paramount importance.

At no point in your career will you work in isolation. Year to year, decade to decade, the same people will crop up personally and professionally. Whether that is other stage managers, directors, designers, crew members, actors, producers, or anyone else you can think of, maintaining strong relationships with your colleagues will make for a more fruitful and positive work life. This will also make life that much easier, as eliminating more and more unknowns as you move in to various shows. Stepping onto a show already knowing three to five of the people you will be working with will immediately build a level of confidence from the outset. Feeling like you are on home turf can completely change your demeanor and your ability to successfully manage a show. Uncertainty breeds stress, and the less uncertainty you feel the more likely it is that you will appear calm and collected throughout the process. These relationships can also turn into some of the best friendships you will ever have.

Building a strong team dynamic

Stage management teams can consist of anywhere from two to four people, sometimes more depending on the complexity of the show, with the Stage Manager charged with leading that group. Ideally the team will have a certain amount of independence and individuality, but it's also important that, as a group, you can present a united front. Getting to know your team, their strengths, weaknesses, and interests is going to go a long way to building a cohesive unit. Honoring who people are and trying to make sure that the work they're doing plays to their strengths will help to create a more fulfilling working environment. For instance, if one of your ASMs also has an interest in costume design, it would make a lot of sense to have them oversee the running of wardrobe for the show. Their active interest and knowledge base will only better serve the production. There are always going to be situations where people will be asked to do things that they don't want to do but tempering those as much as possible will lead to happier colleagues. It is also important to balance the work load of the team as assignments are made. Try not to overburden one person while giving a much easier track to another. Equality across the team is going to help with morale.

Leading a team is not about having people follow you but, rather, about getting people to want to work with you. Fostering a collaborative spirit among the Stage Managers will support a greater bond, to create the internal support structure discussed earlier. Many times teams are assembled by a producer, where the Stage Manager has no input as to who they're working with. This may mean that you're going to be working with people that you have very little in common with personally. Finding common ground is important but if you can't, try to find the joy and humor in your differences. As talked about with the characteristics of Stage Managers, humor is incredibly important for the success of anyone in this profession. If you have an Oscar and Felix (from Neil Simon's *The Odd Couple*) dynamic with other members of the stage management team let that be okay. Don't try and change them to suit your preferences but rather let playfulness with those differences unite you.

The other critically important person the Stage Manager needs to develop a positive relationship with is the Producer. At the end of the day, the Producer is the one that is going to be providing work in the future. This may sound mercenary but it is the reality of the business. Sometimes directors will get to choose the Stage Manager they're going to be working with, but unless they are local to where the show is being produced it is rare that a producer will fly someone in. Often producers will assemble a few Stage Manager options for a director to select from. You want the Producer to trust and feel comfortable enough with you that you land on that list. This relationship becomes even more critical when working in a union setting. Because Stage Managers are represented by the same union as actors, there can be a certain amount of reticence on the Producer's part when they work with someone new. The Stage Manager is charged with making sure that certain union rules are followed, to protect the working conditions of the actors. As the de facto union presence in the rehearsal room, the Stage Manager/Producer relationship can be strained. The Producer needs to know that the Stage Manager has the best interests of the production in mind and will be able to accurately follow union regulation, without making them the focal point of how a project is run.

Following the rules is very important but the way in which that is presented is going to make the difference between a good relationship with the Producers and a bad one. Showing a level of personal investment in the project can make all the difference in your relationship. This is especially true if working in nonprofit theaters. You may see a bit of a shift in for-profit operations where the art that's being produced has a greater personal financial significance to the Producer and the investors. In nonprofit theatre the onus on the company is to make enough money to continue to produce work but also to serve a specific audience and honor a mission statement that the company has. Showing a personal investment to serve that mission helps to ensure that the Producer knows you have a commitment to the work above the paycheck.

The imperative to develop positive relationships with people in the industry certainly extends to the crew and the designers. Over the lifespan of a career designers are going to pop up over and over again, and having a good reputation is going to help you in every situation. It is less common but getting jobs from the recommendations of designers is not unheard of. These often come from lighting designers looking for a competent show caller for a special event or the like. Developing close working relationships with the design teams is not only good for an individual production, but for the health of your career.

Patience and communication

It may sound cliché but the most fundamentally important part of conflict resolution is communication. This is true both in resolving an active conflict and in preempting one from starting in the first place. One of the best ways to develop conflict resolution skills and techniques is to work with children. That statement is not meant to sound derogatory towards the professionals that work in the theatre, and it certainly should not suggest that the Stage Manager should treat their colleagues as children. However, working with children can reveal many of the basic behavior patterns that are universal among humans. A five-year-old throwing a temper tantrum because someone won't share, is rooted in the same fundamental concerns, insecurities, and frustrations that are present in a fifty-year-old who is in conflict with a collaborator because they cannot agree on how best to execute an idea. These two scenarios, while vastly different in many ways, are firmly rooted in the same emotional place for these individuals. Both feel unheard and both feel like they are not able to achieve what they think they should be able to.

In both situations, with the five-year-old and the fifty-year-old, the best thing you can do is start from a place of really listening to their concerns. Hearing what they have to say and allowing them to voice what's bothering them about a given situation will open the door to a productive dialogue starting. Making them feel that someone cares about their concerns and that their voice matters is what will allow you to steer the conversation to a (hopefully) satisfactory conclusion. Never take for granted the power of someone feeling like they are not being ignored.

Patience is paramount for a Stage Manager. Of all the strong personality traits that a successful Stage Manager needs to have, patience is the one tool in the toolbox that they cannot do without. It's tough to be put in a situation where you are asked to manage many different personalities, all trying to accomplish something that they have a strong personal investment in. What tends to separate the reward from the struggle is how patient you are. No matter how frustrating a process can be, wait for that one moment that makes it all worthwhile.

I can point to one specific example that has never left me. A few years ago I was working on a production of a musical at a major concert venue. The pop star who was playing the male lead was staged to make his way out on to the passerelle, a low wall that extends out into the audience. For this moment, I had to cue some crew members to set scenery on the passerelle after the actor passed by. As I was crouched out in the house in front of the passerelle, the actor started to make his way out. I started to hear rumbling behind me. When I turned, I saw these teenage girls in the seats right behind me. They saw that he was coming and the look of elation and excitement on their faces has stuck with me since. Through all the struggle and frustration that goes into putting on a show, the final personality you have to remember to manage is the audience itself. While the Director and writer may be the ones that conceive of the show you are working on, the Stage Manager has the unique pleasure of getting to be responsible for actually making the performance happen each night. When you can see how you have impacted an audience, cherish it, because at the end of the day that is why we do the job.

7

Role of the Stage Manager: Opera

Stories from the front lines

Opera had always been a bit of a mystery to me. My first introduction to opera was during my undergraduate years, so when I was first approached about working on an opera project I found it very intimidating. Those first forays into the operatic world helped to build the foundation for what would later become a medium I truly love working in. For me, the most intimidating part of working in opera for the first time was the idea of reading music. I am not a trained musician. I played a little piano and clarinet as a child but I had long forgotten everything I had learned by the time I was expected to step into an opera rehearsal room. Thankfully, my very first time working in opera did not require the same level of involvement in the music that my later professional opera work would. I was lucky in that moment that I was given the opportunity to brush up my music-reading skills in a nonthreatening and low-intensity way. Flash forward five years and I found myself saying yes to an internship with the Los Angeles Opera. For those unaware, LA Opera is considered one of the United States' "big houses." These include organizations like San Francisco Opera and The Metropolitan Opera. Needless to say, I was nervous.

My first week of preparations on *La Boheme* was one of the most terrifying of my professional career. I felt confident in my abilities as a Stage Manager, but I was entering a world I truly had no frame of reference for. The pressure to excel was high and I was not sure I would be able to live up to the challenge. That first week

I was handed a seventy-five-page document from the last time this production was produced by the company, and told I was responsible for maintaining it with absolute accuracy. This terrifying document is referred to as the "who, what, where." This is a piece of running paperwork I had never even heard of before.

I was also faced with a more formal and hierarchical organizational structure than I had experienced in theatre. I was used to a very relaxed and collaborative atmosphere and I now had to adapt to a new expectation of what my professional behavior should be. It was all quite jarring for a student of the theatre.

Organization

Depending on one's background, opera can be a scary thing to contemplate stepping into. For musicians-turned-Stage-Managers, the transition is a bit easier. For those coming from theatre, it is a whole other world. From the outside, opera is grand, opulent, and just plain big. The productions usually include hundreds of people, massive sets, intricate costumes, and a full orchestra. It is an incredible sight to behold, but as a Stage Manager it's also a huge responsibility. Like any performing arts discipline, opera comes with its own culture and traditions, so learning those is going to be the first step settling into this whole new world.

The organizational structure for opera bears some resemblance to the theatre but differs in certain significant ways. As with any show, there is a team of people intimately involved in mounting the show. Figure 1 is a basic chart that breaks down the staff present in the rehearsal room.

Music Director/Conductor

The Music Director, in an opera company, functions very much the same way as an Artistic Director does for a theatre. This position is, generally, a staff position or post that a conductor will assume for a period of time. They are charged with the artistic oversight for the programming of the company. During their tenure at a given company, the Music Director will often have some kind of hallmark that becomes associated with them, as their personal artistic preferences influence the programming of the company.

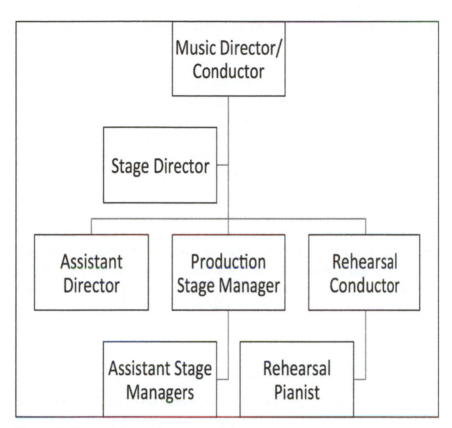

Figure 1 Opera rehearsal room staff chart.

For example, if the Music Director of the company declares that as long as he holds his position the company will be a Wagner-focused company, this means that the works of Richard Wagner—some of the world's most difficult to produce operas—will remain an important part of the fabric of the company's programming for the duration of their tenure. Like a theatre's Artistic Director, the length of a Music Director's tenure is often determined by their own personal professional choices and the financial success of the seasons they oversee. Also similar to the theatrical model, the Music Director is frequently contractually obligated to participate in a certain number of productions each season, in this case as the Conductor. From time to time, the Music Director will also officially carry the title of Artistic Director, or the role is partially split with another artist, who will carry a title like General Director.

Every opera production requires a conductor, whether that person is also the company's Music Director or not. As noted earlier, the Conductor (or

Maestro) holds the final word on all artistic matters on a production. The rationale behind this stems from the fact that opera, like orchestra, is all about the music. The lavish production elements, and even the story telling, come second to the singers and musicians presenting the composition in the most musically effective way possible. This means that the Conductor's vision of what the production should sound like will always take precedence over the aesthetic considerations of the Stage Director or design team. While this seems like a striking difference from the theatre, when you think about it, it is not so different from the mentality that a director's chief responsibility is to present the playwright's work in the clearest and most faithful way possible.

This is not meant to suggest that opera is not a collaborative art form, it absolutely is. It is, however, important to note the difference in priorities. Where in musical theatre a production might be able to get away with a lead who is a phenomenal actor but only an adequate signer, opera has the reverse mentality; the singing comes first.

Director/Stage Director

Looking at the credits for an opera production, there will likely be one of three terms listed after the Conductor: "Director," "Stage Director," and "Production by" all relate to the same basic position but do have slight differences from each other.

As with the theatre, the Director is charged with conceiving a cohesive vision for a production and working to guide the cast and design team towards its execution. Unlike in theatre, however, this artistic vision has to be in collaboration with—and in support—of the Conductor's vision for the aural interpretation of the score. This has both positive and negative aspects. The positive is that it allows the Stage Director greater freedom to visually interpret the production as he/she sees fit. Often with theatre, Directors will be restricted by the given circumstances of a play. Time period, theatrical style, and location are all critical concerns for most theatrical productions. Opera, however, tends to function in much the same way Shakespeare is produced today. When charged with directing a new production of a Shakespearean play, you have the option to create something very traditional and adhere to specifics provided in the text, or you can take the opportunity to reinterpret the circumstances of the play in order to draw greater meaning from the text. This interpretational freedom, and the priority being on the performance of the music rather than acting or storytelling, is why opera has become known for its lavish productions, and often avant-garde approach.

The title "Production by" takes the role of Director a step further. When someone is credited with the words "Production by," it usually will mean that they conceived the entire production. That credit normally refers to auteur directors who design the scenery, costumes, lighting, and any other combination of elements of the production. Opera is generally so expensive to produce that a global rental model has developed where most companies will produce only one to two new productions each season. The rest of the season is comprised of remounting that company's stock of productions or renting one from another company. This is different from the touring model of theatre and even differs from the rental model often seen in the productions of musicals by Civic Light Opera companies. When an opera production is rented, it often will come with the requirement that the full production is remounted, down to the smallest detail. This is the other scenario in which "Production by" is used. The production's original Director will now be billed as the conceiver of the production, assuming that person is not going to be on hand to direct the remounted show.

It is in these instances where the term *Stage Director* comes into play. The Stage Director is usually the director who has been hired to oversee the remounting of an existing production. They will be charged with the same responsibilities of a normal director, but rather than trying to execute their own artistic concept they are executing another director's, based on the original realization of that vision. As a necessity there will always be a certain game of telephone that is played in this process, unless the Stage Director worked on the original mounting of the production. There is some room for reinterpretation in these instances but it is usually very limited and, depending on the strictness of the rental contract, may feel nonexistent.

Assistant Director

The role of the Assistant Director, or AD, is probably the most dramatically different from what is found in the theatre. The AD in opera often functions as a bridge between the production team and the artistic team. Depending on the opera company, the AD can be responsible for everything from taking blocking notation and staging large chorus scenes for the Director, to generating the rehearsal schedule and communicating it to the Stage Manager. This can be very surprising to theatre Stage Managers coming into the opera rehearsal process blind.

One of the AD's primary responsibilities on an opera production is the accurate recording of all the staged movement. This is critical for the rental and remounting process (discussed earlier) to work well. If a production has an AD who does not take clear and complete notes, the next company to produce the show will have a very difficult road ahead of them. In addition to traditional blocking notation, the AD also will create the official character scene breakdown for the production in advance of the start of rehearsals and maintain it throughout the process. The preliminary rehearsal schedule and any updates, maintenance of the show after opening, integration of covers (understudies), and brush-up rehearsals all fall to the AD to oversee in the world of opera.

In addition to having to maintain a positive and productive relationship with the Director, the AD must build a strong partnership with the Stage Manager. In many ways, this is the most critical relationship for each of these production team members to build. They will not only be working closely throughout the rehearsal and performance process, they must rely on the other's support and accuracy, as operas tend to be enormous undertakings that they are both responsible for overseeing.

Stage Manager/Production Stage Manager

In opera, the Stage Manager's function is very similar to their role in the theatre. As with the theatre, an opera Stage Manager manages a team of ASMs, calls the show, runs room rehearsals, and serves as the primary liaison between the creative team and the production staff and crew that will make a show happen on the stage. As discussed, the AD assumes a certain number of the responsibilities that would be assigned to the Stage Manager in theatre; however, this does not mean that the Stage Manager is completely removed from all involvement in these tasks. Generally, the Stage Manager will still take their own blocking notes, with special focus on entrances and exits. Sometimes there is simply too much happening on stage for one person to record on their own, and so having the AD, Stage Manager, and ASMs record this information can be extremely helpful. It is important to remember though that the AD is maintaining the official record of the show. If there is a discrepancy between the Stage Manager's notes and the AD's, the AD's notes will be deferred to.

The title *Production Stage Manager* often refers to a formal staff appointment in opera. Many companies have a resident team of Stage Managers that they work with regularly and are led by a full-time PSM, who will manage the hiring of Stage Managers and ASMs. Depending on the company structure, the PSM will also handle the hiring of ADs. This may seem like an odd addition to the PSM's responsibilities, but it only reinforces the fact that in opera the AD is considered to be a member of the production staff, and is really a member of the stage management team. Like the Music Director, the PSM is also often contractually obligated to stage manage a certain number of shows per season. Depending on the number of shows in a season, the schedule, and the complexity of the productions a PSM may even stage manage all shows in the season. A full-time PSM will often participate in the advance planning for a season and assist the Director of Production or other members of the administration to identify the potential needs and impact of a given production. This role, and the company continuity it creates, is a great asset in the world of opera that is rarely found in theatre.

It is one thing to have a strong relationship with a company as a freelancer, but it is quite another to actually be a full-time employee of the company. That being said, the closer relationship to the company can also pose potential problems, depending on the attitudes of the staff or artists you are working with. The concept of the "company man" and the concerns it tends to raise can create a precarious work environment for the PSM to navigate. Stage Managers, in general, are asked to split their loyalties between the Producer who hires them and the creative/production team they are working with on a given project. This is made more difficult when they are a full-time employee of the Producer. As a result, the PSM must walk a fine line in the dynamic they build with the creative team, because they essentially become a representative of the more ominous version of "management" in the rehearsal room. This is not how most PSMs see themselves and so they must work that much harder to ensure that the artists they are working with see that they are engaged and supportive of the project, no matter who is signing their checks. This also makes the AD's relationship with the Director and PSM even more important as they are able to represent a more unbiased figure to the Director.

Assistant Stage Manager

The Assistant Stage Manager, or ASM, functions in opera in the same way as in the theatre. That role includes supporting the Stage Manager in the running of both the rehearsals and performances of a given production. They will be the Stage Manager's eyes and ears backstage and will keep track of all props, shifts in scenery, and any other technical cues that will occur on the stage and directly affect the performers. The major distinguishing factor in the ASM's role in opera, as opposed to theatre, is the calling of entrance cues. In opera, due to the often repetitive nature of music, the cast is not charged with making entrances of their own accord. The ASMs and Stage Manager are all expected to be following along in the score throughout the show, so as the cast is not following along it becomes the responsibility of the stage management team to cue cast members to make their entrances. In fact, in many situations, cast members are firmly not allowed to enter the stage without being cued by a Stage Manager. The strictness of the adherence to this cultural rule varies from company to company and artist to artist. Some singers will rely completely on the ASMs to give them their cues, while others will wave off ASMs who try to. It is important to understand the expectations of the company you are working for and to carefully read the personality of the artist you are working with, as this part of the job can get touchy.

As with theatre, the level of autonomy that an ASM receives on an opera production varies. If there is a large group of ASMs, the Stage Manager may completely turn over the running of the deck to them. If there is only one ASM, the Stage Manager may split the role with the ASM as well as call the show. Being clear about what team dynamic is desired is an important part of getting started on any new show.

The process

The rehearsal process for an opera closely mirrors the theatre, with some notable differences. Some of this information may seem obvious or redundant from earlier chapters, but going through the process in order and in detail will provide a clearer understanding of what to expect when jumping into an opera.

Preproduction/prep week

As in theatre, how early the SM actively joins a production will depend on their personal schedule, the company they are working for, the size of the company's full-time staff, and, most importantly, the union status of the company. As with AEA, the American Guild of Musical Artists (AGMA) will establish the rules for the length of the prep week and the pay scale for the time spent working prior to the start of rehearsals.

There are two distinct methods of prepping for an opera and they are a direct result of the culture of rentals and remounts. In the case of a rental/ remount situation, the company is provided with the archival paperwork from the last mounting of the production. This means the stage management staff walk into prep with a significant amount of information to be able to acquaint themselves with the show. The availability of this paperwork generates an expectation that the stage management team will be able to walk into the first rehearsal ready to make the rehearsal work without direction from the Director. In this model, the goal in prep should be to get to the point that you can get every artist on stage at the right time, with the right prop, and in the right costume so that the Director only worries about staging the artist once they have entered the stage. The big question becomes "How do you accomplish this level of preparedness?" There are a few documents that will get you and the overall team ready to go.

The score

Where in theatre you work from a script, in opera you will always work from a score. This is why the Stage Manager and ASMs must be able to, at least comfortably, follow music. Many Stage Managers and ASMs in opera are former singers or musicians and are proficient in reading music. Usually, if available, the team will be provided with a "piano vocal" or "piano reduction" score. This means that the full Conductor's score (which includes every note for every instrument in the orchestra) has been distilled into a simplified version that can be played on the piano and still give the same basic effect of the full version to rehearse with. A reduction is much easier to read than a full conductor's score, and is much shorter since more music can fit on a single page. The Stage Manager will prepare their score in advance of the first rehearsal as best they can. Generally the volume of archival material on an existing production is so immense it does not make sense to try to transfer all off it into the score, so the most important points must be identified. For the Stage Manager, the most essential information to have on hand in their score is going to be anything that they will be calling. This means if they are provided with the light cues from the previous production it may be wise to indicate them in your score. Any scenic shifts, automation cues, rail cues, etc., are going be critical so that when asked where something is supposed to happen, or where it happened last time, that information can be provided quickly and accurately. Some Stage Managers will include entrance/exit information in their score from the get go. Some will only include entrance information because that is what their team is going to be cueing during the rehearsal, and should they have to step in to help they need to have it on hand.

For ASMs, the score preparation is going to be a little different. The ASM's primary responsibility during normal room rehearsals is going to be to cue artists for their entrances and manage props and rehearsal costumes. If the team of ASMs is large enough, each will most likely be assigned one side of the stage or the other. This means that the Stage Right ASM is going to be responsible for everything that happens Stage Right, and the same for Stage Left, Up Stage, Under the Stage, etc. Once they have their assignment, most ASMs will put their focus during prep on making sure that all information related to their side of the stage is in their score. This means all entrances and exits, as well as prop and wardrobe presets, scene shifts, etc. Depending on the situation, it may also be important to include some amount of information about the opposite side of the stage in the score as well. It is a personal choice how to organize this, as long as whatever method chosen by the ASM translates into a strong confidence in their ability to manage the things they are charged with beginning on the first day of rehearsal.

The who, what, where

The "who, what, where," or WWW, is a document that is applicable to every theatrical discipline but it is most common in opera. It is another version of running paperwork, but also serves as a complete archive of a production, distilled into a grid. WWWs record every entrance and exit that occurs in a show. In addition, they include the costume a character is wearing, the prop they carry, any onstage technical cues, wardrobe changes, and even important lighting and projection cues. Different companies utilize WWWs in different ways. For some they are solely an archival tool and are not used in the actual running of the production, instead replaced with individual paperwork for each department. For others, they serve as the only running paperwork, or at least the master source from which the paperwork for each department is pulled.

The WWW is normally laid out in a grid pattern, and there are certain hard-and-fast rules as to what is to be included.

1 Placement
Placement refers to the moment in the score where something occurs. This can be an entrance, exit, prop handoff, technical cue, etc. Placements

in scores are usually formatted in the following way: Page/System/Bar. One would hope that everyone working on the production has the same version of the score to work from. This means the first portion of the placement, the page, should be consistent across the whole production and creative teams, as well as the cast. For those who are not musicians or singers and are unfamiliar with the formatting of sheet music, the terms *system* and *bar* may be foreign. When looking at a page of sheet music from a piano reduction, you will note that it is usually broken up into a number of large, horizontal sections. Each of these sections is referred to as a "system." In a full conductor's score, often, a single system will take up an entire page because it contains all the instruments in the orchestra listed all the way down the page. Because a reduction is only for a piano, multiple systems can fit on a single page. Generally, there are between three to five systems per page, but this will vary depending on the piece of music being looked at. Within each system there will be vertical lines that break up the system into segments. These are called bars. For a Stage Manager, these provide helpful markers to be able to easily reference where in the music something occurs. When writing a placement, the page, followed by the system, followed by the bar are indicated; for example, 57/2/4.

There are variations in this format. From time to time, Stage Managers will use the word "last" in place of a system or bar as a shorthand, instead of counting out everything. Keep in mind that "last" should only be used in place of the system if it will also be used in place of the bar. For example, 57/2/last, 57/last/last or 57/last are all acceptable, but 57/last/4 is not. Also remember that using last will usually mean the end of the last bar rather than the beginning. If this seems confusing or convoluted, or fear it might confuse the next person who will have to use that paperwork, it will be safer to just count everything out. If there is a need to be extremely specific, indicating the beat within the bar where something occurs can be done by adding that number after the bar; for example, 57/2/4/three. The use of that fourth number is rare and should be saved for very specific moments because, as with any theatrical discipline, once you are in the performance there is going to need to be room to breathe, and rarely will anything happen on the beat you have dictated.

2 Time

Timings are incredibly important. They help the crew and future Stage Managers understand the flow of the show in a much clearer way. They can be difficult in theatre because there is usually no complete recording of a show to take timings from, and productions vary so dramatically that the only reliable timings must be taken during a technical rehearsal or performance. They can also be done during a final room rehearsal, but in all of these scenarios the Stage Manager has numerous other things to focus on.

Marking timings in the score generally means following along and putting a time indication in the music score every thirty seconds. This seems like a lot but it will help immensely in the long run. Doing this not only helps you get acquainted with the music, it also means that when it comes time to put together the paperwork, a huge amount of the work has already been done. Having the time indications in the score is incredibly helpful during rehearsals and performance as well. Due to the long running time of operas, many people will come to ask how much time remains in an act and having the timings readily available in the score will mean the answer is always on hand. In a union situation, where overtime is an issue, it is immensely helpful to be able to have rough timings to help guide the planning of rehearsals and course correcting if things are running long.

3 Who

The first of the "W"s, "Who" refers to the character/cast/crew member that will execute the "what." For the WWW, it is good to get into the habit of indicating not only the character name (which will matter for the next production team to use the paperwork) but also the performer's name. Generally, the format for this column is as follows: *Character Name (First Initial. Last Name)*; for example, *James (M. Vitale)*. The logic behind this format relates to the hit-by-a-bus rule. If someone else had to pick up this document and take over, they should know the character they are looking for, and also be able to refer to the performer by their title (Mr., Ms., Mrs., etc.) and their last name.

When creating the WWW, always remember that it is for someone else. It is going to be used by the rest of the stage management team as well as by other teams for many years to come. Always think about communication in these terms. While a shortcut may make sense to you, it may not to the next person to use your paperwork. This means that being specific about how people are ordered for entrances and exits does matter. If there is a large group entering and they are listed arbitrarily, no one is going to be able replicate the entrance correctly, without taking some time to figure things out. You will use someone else's WWW to create your score, so remember that someone else will be using yours to create theirs. Plan appropriately.

4 *What/Where*

This area is self-explanatory. These last two "W"s are coupled for clarity and refer to the action to be executed and where it takes place; for example, *Enter SR*. For clarity, it is often helpful to group things by both placement/timing and action. If you have multiple people entering from a single location at the same moment, placing your border lines around that complete list instead of around each line will help to clarify what is happening. See the WWW examples on the Companion Website for a representation of how this would look.

5 *Costume*

Whether technical cues are included in the WWW or not, including information about costumes is a must. From a purely practical standpoint this will allow the stage management team to spot-check that people are dressed correctly for their entrances. This is particularly useful for room rehearsals when there will not be wardrobe crew support and you will often be asked if a performer is wearing a jacket, hat, or other item in a given moment. This also helps to track wardrobe developments during the rehearsal process and easily communicate the information to the wardrobe department.

6 *Prop*

The rationale for including prop information with an entrance or exit is essentially the same as including costume details. Having the details of what items an artist should be carrying for an entrance, or will be bringing off when they exit, will allow you to ensure they are fully ready when you cue them on to the stage. It also, again, creates a progressive method for tracking prop movement during the rehearsals and turns that into running paperwork for the crew.

Room rehearsals

Different opera companies will have different versions of how rehearsals will be set up, but there are certain standards that guide the way the rehearsals are structured. Most companies build their rehearsals around a three-hour session format. This means that a single, complete rehearsal is three hours in length. However, more than one three-hour rehearsal is permitted in a day. In theatre, a single rehearsal is thought of as the span of the whole day; for example, a straight six refers to a six-hour rehearsal, which is the entire rehearsal day. There will be no other rehearsal scheduled after the straight six concludes. In opera, it is permissible to have a morning session of three hours, followed by lunch, and then an afternoon session of another three hours. These are thought of as individual rehearsals, or services, and not as one six-hour rehearsal day with a meal break. This may seem like an unimportant distinction but it becomes critical in how you schedule rehearsals and work with the union rules associated with the span of the day. There are, of course, variations in this standard from company to company and even exceptions, such as having a four-hour rehearsal if that is the only rehearsal that will occur on that day.

During the course of one of these three-hour sessions there is a requirement to take thirty minutes of break. These thirty minutes can be broken up, however, as long as a break is taken no more than ninety minutes after the start of the rehearsal. For efficiency, many shows will just take a twenty-minute break after ninety minutes and then end the rehearsal ten minutes early.

In an opera rehearsal room hierarchy is incredibly important to keep in mind. If the Conductor is not in the room, the Director dictates how the rehearsal progresses. If the Conductor is in the room, everything will go through them, despite the fact that room (or staging) rehearsals are considered the Director's rehearsals. Usually, passing rehearsal requests through the Conductor during these rehearsals is simply a courtesy and sign of respect, but occasionally the Conductor will have very specific ideas of what should occur. As discussed before, the music is the single highest priority in opera, so if the person charged with overseeing the music for the production has a strong desire to rehearse something that will likely take precedence over the staging. Again, this is a rare occurrence but it is important to be aware that it is something that does happen from time to time and you should not be surprised when it does.

Tech

The technical rehearsal process for opera follows a similar model to musical theatre. Opera productions are often large and extravagant but, beyond the scenery, props, and costumes, the single most significant element that is added during tech is the orchestra. Prior to the technical rehearsal process the show has been rehearsed with a piano, but now comes the introduction of twenty, thirty, forty, even seventy musicians to the mix and the concept of "Conductor is king" kicks into full gear. In order to give both the Conductor and Director the time they need to make the show the best it can be, the tech process is broken into eight different types of rehearsals. Depending on the production and the company, not all of these types may be used but they are terms that are heard over and over and you should understand what they mean.

1   *Orchestra rehearsal*
    The orchestra rehearsal is exactly what it sounds like. It is a rehearsal for the orchestra only. This is the equivalent of a room rehearsal but for the musicians. These will often be held in a rehearsal room or studio rather than on stage, but if the stage is available they may happen there.

2   *Sitzprobe*
    Sitzprobe is a German word that means "seated rehearsal." The sitzprobe, or "sitz," is a practical necessity in order to bring everything together in an opera. A sitz is usually the first time that the singers and the orchestra will rehearse together. The preference is to hold this rehearsal in the theater so that the Conductor can begin to get a sense of the acoustic balance they need to create between the music and the voices, however this may be impossible, in which case a rehearsal room will suffice. During this rehearsal, the singers will sit in chairs and then step forward when it is their moment to sing. This is purely a music rehearsal and stage management need only ensure that the appropriate people are in the room at the right time. There is no cueing of artists, beyond calling them to the stage. Sitzes are also common in musical theatre, where space and time allow.

3   *Wandelprobe*
    Based on the definition of sitzprobe, you can probably guess the meaning of "wandelprobe." In a "wandel" the cast will go through some amount of their blocking during the course of the rehearsal. This can mean everything from doing every single movement to simply standing in the vicinity of the location where they will sing a particular portion of the piece from. From time to time it will make much more sense to have this be a purely musical rehearsal, with the cast on their feet. Usually this occurs when the set has multiple levels or the singers will

be performing from locations where it will make it difficult for them to see the Conductor or will change the overall acoustical balance of the performance. A "wandel" is never assumed to be occurring so it is important to clarify with the Conductor, Director, and Producers whether one will take place. Often, a sitz will be on the schedule and that sitz will evolve into a wandel out of necessity. In the case of a wandel, stage management will likely need to cue entrances and exits.

4 *Piano tech*
The piano tech is the first opportunity for the design team, director, and cast to begin putting the technical elements of the production together into something cohesive. Generally, these rehearsals will be conducted by the rehearsal Conductor and the Director will be driving the bus. Efficiency is critical in these rehearsals because this is going to be the only comfortable opportunity to stop and repeat sections of the show to get everything right. Once the orchestra is introduced, it's important to not be caught in a situation where the technical elements are holding things up.

5 *Piano dress*
As with any dress rehearsal, the piano dress wants to be as much of a run through as possible. You have to maintain realistic expectations, of course, but the more fluid the run is the more everyone will gain from it. This is usually the first time the actual costumes are introduced into the process, and as a result there may be holds to rehearse quick changes and the like, but any wardrobe department will tell you that they will benefit the most from a real time run of the show. It is also important to remember that this rehearsal will be the last before introducing the orchestra. This will be the last rehearsal where the Director will be able to tweak and fine-tune the production without having to get the Conductor onboard to stop and fix something. This will also be the last chance the Stage Manager has to ask to run something for themselves.

6 *Orchestra tech*
The orchestra tech will be the first introduction of the orchestra into the tech process. By the time the first orchestra tech comes along the show should be ready to run; at least that will be the expectation from the Conductor and orchestra. At no point should technical needs hold up rehearsals once the orchestra has arrived. This may seem

unreasonable for a rehearsal labeled "tech," but there is one significant reason for this: money. Aside from the music-first culture of the opera world, it is just expensive to put on an opera, and when you add in an orchestra of thirty to forty players the operating costs jump dramatically. In musical theatre, pit bands can consist of as few as one to four players or can grow to twenty-five to thirty, but those occasions are rare. In opera the standard is for a larger orchestra and that means, on a per-service pay structure, fewer rehearsals will be scheduled with the musicians. Having the show in good condition before they arrive means the Conductor is able to maximize his or her rehearsal time with the orchestra. This expectation puts a great deal of pressure on the stage management team to make the show work no matter what.

7 *Orchestra dress*
   The orchestra dress rehearsals are full dresses with the orchestra. These should be able to run in show conditions, with the only stopping being due to the Conductor wanting to make musical corrections. There is always the possibility that this won't be the case, but that is the aim for the team as it works through the technical rehearsal process.

8 *Final dress*
   This is no different than any other final dress. The goal here is to run the show as though it was a performance. As in theatre, many companies will have an invited final dress, so that it functions like a preview performance. This is always ideal because it gives the cast a chance to feel the energy and response of an audience before opening. Unlike theatre, opera rarely has a preview period so the final dress is normally the only opportunity to have an audience before opening.

Performance

In all forms of theatrical performance, the health of the performers is paramount. In order to have a show, the cast has to actually be able to go out on stage and deliver their best work. In opera this manifests itself in the performance schedule for a show. Jump online and take a look at the website for one of the major opera companies. Looking at their calendar, you will note that there may be one or two performances of a given show in a week. The reason for this is the vocal health of the singers.

Almost without exception, operas are performed without amplification. This means that the singers are having to project their voice above the sound of a full orchestra and try to fill a massive theater. Many opera companies perform in traditional theaters, not concert halls or opera houses whose acoustics are designed to support the unamplified voice. This means that those singers have an even greater struggle to overcome. It may seem simple enough to just add some microphones and save everyone the trouble, but this issue also has its roots in the cultural traditions of the art form itself. The idea of amplifying opera singers is a taboo notion and must always be approached very carefully. Singing without a microphone is a matter of pride for many singers and suggesting it implies that they are unable to effectively do their job.

Aside from the normal run of show duties for the stage management team, there are a few special tasks that relate directly to opera. The most critical of these are "*pages*." It is in "paging" that the importance of the thirty-second timings and cueing artists onto the stage come together. Paging refers to making announcements on the backstage PA system, often called a paging system. For operas, it is expected that the Stage Manager, or one of the ASMs, will call artists to the stage roughly five minutes prior to their entrance. This five minutes allows them to put on any costume elements they may have removed (a jacket, hat, etc.) and make the walk from the dressing room to the stage. The five-minute rule is flexible and should be adjusted based on circumstance. If someone needs some extra warning due to costume difficulties, or even just slow responsiveness, back-up the call appropriately. It is not advisable to shorten the call, however. If there is an artist who is very responsive and really only needs a two-minute call, still call them at five minutes. Let them adjust their response time rather than adjusting the call. This is simply because neither of you want to hit the day where you call them at two minutes and they had been distracted and now do not have the time they need to get to their place. Moral of the story: feel free to call people earlier than five minutes, never call them later.

The top-of-show sequence

Operas follow a similar top-of-show structure to orchestras. Along with the standard house to half, cell-phone announcement, and house-out, there are a few special features that occur when working in classical music. The orchestra must always tune and this practical action has become a featured moment for any operatic performance. Following the tuning of the orchestra, the Conductor will make a formal entrance into the pit to a massive round of applause. Traditionally the Conductor will step up so that they are fully visible to the audience, and bow. Depending on the situation, the Conductor may also encourage the orchestra to stand to be acknowledged before actually starting the performance. From here they will start conducting and the show progresses like any other. This whole process is repeated at the intermission.

For Stage Managers who enjoy working on shows with grandeur and spectacle, opera is a great road to go down. The world of opera is very different from that of theatre but, in a lot of ways, can be a nice break. The rules and formality allow the Stage Manager to be boxed into their responsibilities, so it can serve as a nice reprieve from the "everything-to-everyone" mentality that exists in the theatre. These are of course broad statements and won't apply to every opera company, but are relatively consistent across the board. Opera also can be a great bridge into the world of music, in general. There is enough overlap between opera and theatre, and opera and music, to allow Stage Managers to test the water in opera, and then decide about moving to the other disciplines.

8

Role of the Stage Manager: Music

Stage management in the world of music is wholly different from any of the disciplines discussed so far. From classical to pop to rock and roll, live music performance requires a very different mentality from the Stage Manager. While in other mediums the Stage Manager has an active role to play in creating the world of a performance, with music the majority of the Stage Manager's activity is focused on the work that happens in advance of curtain. For those Stage Managers who identify strongly as technicians, music is a great career path to explore.

In music, generally many of the elements associated with theatrical stage management are stripped away. With the exception of major pop acts, who embrace theatricality with scenery, costumes, and even dance, most music performances remain focused on the musician and the music being played instead of ancillary elements of production. Because the vast majority of music performance does not include these elements, the Stage Manager is freed up to absorb certain responsibilities that are normally associated with production management or line producing. The goal of supporting the artist's ability to create and perform in a safe space remains the same, but the method of accomplishing this goal changes.

Classical music

The world of classical music has a culture and tradition all of its own. There are a certain amount of similarities between the orchestra world and the opera world, but when it comes to the role of the Stage Manager they could not be more different. Classical music is one of the oldest performing art forms and, unlike theatre, the formalities and traditions of the institution have not evolved dramatically since its emergence. There is a very clear hierarchy in and among not only the conductor but the orchestra members themselves. One of the important differences between the orchestral world and other, more theatrical, models is that there is really no place for the Stage Manager in the hierarchy of the artists. Whereas in theatre or opera the Stage Manager is viewed as a critical and integral part of the process with a specific and integrated role to play in the work that the artists are doing, in the orchestra world the Stage Manager exists almost apart from the artists. While the Stage Manager's responsibilities are clear, their place on the food chain is not, and so they often must find a way to slot into the environment created by each conductor in order to do their job.

Similar to the event world, orchestra Stage Managers are charged with both stage management and production management responsibilities. Unless you're being brought in for a theatrical project, you're likely to be working as a full-time or part-time staff member, dedicated to a specific orchestra. Freelancing as an orchestral Stage Manager is not really a part of the professional landscape. Orchestra musicians work for a specific orchestra for many years, and having a consistent Stage Manager working with the organization allows them to learn the preferences and eccentricities of the musicians and Music Director to create a more comfortable and supportive environment. In addition to getting to know the people, orchestra Stage Managers also develop a greater understanding of the facilities and resources available to the organization. These can include the crew, venue, instrument stock, and organizational structure of the company.

Again, hierarchy plays a major role in the world of orchestral music so developing an understanding of the pecking order and priorities of the company is crucial. In many ways, treating the various artists they will be working with in the appropriate manner is one of the single most important jobs an orchestra Stage Manager has. Like an opera company, orchestras have a Music Director, who is publicly the final voice on the artistic output of the company. The Music Director is also the principal conductor of the orchestra. They, along with the President and CEO, are the most visible people in an orchestral organization. As with any arts organization, there is a support staff who run the day-to-day operations of the company. Programmers put together the season that will be performed, Personnel Managers oversee the musicians as employees, Operations Managers and Production/Stage Managers oversee the advance and execution of the concerts themselves. Every organization has its own structure and they vary company to company. Because the freelance element is removed from production you will find that each company handles the role of the Stage Manager in its own way.

What is consistent, however, is that the Stage Manager is charged with making sure the orchestra is set appropriately for each concert. Each concert requires some variation in the orchestra's layout but there are some hard and fast rules associated with the setup. Unless you are an orchestra buff you may not have taken the time to really evaluate an orchestra when you have seen one.

The basics of orchestra setup are:

- **The Conductor**
  The Conductor is positioned downstage of the orchestra. It is critical that every musician be able to see the Conductor and they will let you know if there is an obstruction impeding their view. They usually stand on a podium to help make them more visible. The conductor is the headliner of the concert they are conducting and they are treated as such. A lot of the cultural elements of opera hold true here. Whatever the Maestro wants, the Maestro gets. At the end of the day, they are the one who is going to get panned in a bad review, and they are the one who will get the praise if it is good. Their role, in the eye of the public and the hierarchy of the concert, is a kind of hybrid between a lead actor and a director.
- **The strings**
  Directly in front of the Conductor sit the strings. The string sections can be laid out in various configurations but the two most common are (from the conductor's left):

  I first violins, second violins, violas, cellos, and basses behind cellos

  II First violins, cellos, basses behind cellos, violas, and second violins

The string configuration is at the discretion of the conductor. There are two major reasons why a conductor would select one string configuration over another. The first is that the conductor must clearly communicate with the orchestra, and different conductors have preferences on how they will do that. If a conductor is used to having cellos on their right, they will choose the first option and vice versa. Using their personal preference on how things are set up will create a consistency in their ability to perform. The second consideration when it comes to selecting a string configuration is artistic. Different configurations can impact the audience's acoustical experience of the piece being performed. Splitting the violins creates an antiphonal sound, which may support one piece rather than another. If the conductor desires more prominence to the lower string sounds then putting the cellos and basses closer to the audience can make a lot of sense. This is the closest to "staging" that a conductor will come in the world of the orchestra but it can have a monumental effect on the performance.

- **The winds**

  In the center of the orchestra, directly behind the strings, are the woodwinds. The woodwinds are laid out, from the conductor's left: flutes, oboes/English horns, and then directly behind them (again from the conductor's left), clarinets, and bassoons. Again, there is some flexibility here depending on the piece of music and the preferences of the conductor, but this standard layout rarely changes. The biggest fluctuation in the woodwind configuration has to do with the size of the section. For example, if there are no flutes or oboes in a piece the clarinets and bassoon may move down a row.

- **The horns and brass**

  Directly behind the woodwinds is the horns and brass section. The configuration of these instruments is probably the most variable orchestra to orchestra. It is generally laid out: French horns, trumpets, trombones, and tubas. The first French horn is set on center and the section is built going stage right from that. Next to the first French horn is the first trumpet and they are built going stage left with the trombones next to them, followed by the tubas. Brass players are the most likely to have specialized positions called for in the score. It is not uncommon for a piece of music to have offstage brass, and in these circumstances it is usually a conversation between the Conductor, the principal player in the section that is playing offstage, and the Stage Manager about what is possible in the venue that you are performing in. For these offstage moments, conductors and musicians are always looking for a new and creative location to create the sound they want to hear so this can be a fun challenge for the Stage Manager to identify what can be done.

- **The percussion**

  Behind the brass lives the percussion section. Due to the varying size of percussion piece by piece there is always a lot of conversation between the players and the Stage Manager about where they will be set up and how. Due to the dramatic variations in what instruments are required for the percussion section there are not many hard-and-fast rules about their setup. The principal player will work with the section to figure out what is going to work best for them and will then let the Stage Manager know what they would like to do. Depending on the piece, the Conductor may also have some strong opinions about where things should be placed. The most common variable is the presence of more than one set of timpani. Sometimes these will both be set center, and sometimes the Conductor will want an antiphonal sound and split them stage right and left. Because they take up a good-sized footprint, the placement of these will impact how the rest of the section will be set.

- **The keyboards and harp**

  Most of the time, these will function as a unit. The term "keyboards" is the general term that refers to pianos, organs, celeste, harpsichords, and anything else with a keyboard on it. As much as possible, harpists like to play next to the piano and there is a lot of back and forth between their two instruments. If space prohibits this, harps are also often set in front of the piano. As with every section, there are exceptions to the rules here. Certain pieces will require the harps and pianos to be placed in different locations depending on how they will interact with other instruments in the orchestra.

Working with artists

Almost all large orchestras build their seasons around guest conductors and soloists. While the Music Director will be contractually obligated to conduct a certain number of concerts throughout the course of a season, they are usually not required to conduct all of them. As a result, guest conductors are required to fill the gaps. As with any artist, conductors have their specialties. Some are renowned for their artistry with classics like Mozart or Wagner, while others know new music like the back of their hands. Featured soloists provide a "coheadliner" with the conductor that will attract audiences and keep the programming fresh and interesting. All of this means that the Stage Manager is going to have to interact with a variety of rotating artists over the course of a season and years of repeat visits.

Building a positive relationship with these guest artists is equally as important as building a positive relationship with the standing orchestra. Companies have deep relationships with different conductors, soloists, and composers, so these people will be around quite frequently. The hierarchical nature of the orchestral world will also call for them to be treated as VIPs and, depending on the profile of the artist, their presence can cause quite a stir when they arrive. As with any human interaction you are going to run into the loveliest people and the most difficult, and the best thing you can do is to treat everyone with an equal level of respect. Certain people will demand greater accommodations than others but that comes with the territory, so the more flexible and positive you can be the better you will survive a career in this industry. One of the biggest challenges of orchestral stage management, however, is that the presence of these guest VIPs and their preferences are being layered onto a standing group of over one hundred other artists, each with their own needs that must be supported by the Stage Manager.

The orchestra is your constant ensemble. You will develop close working relationships—and even friendships—with many of them and it is important to develop a relationship of mutual respect. Each member of the ensemble is an individual artist in their own right, who has specific needs to do their best work and it is your responsibility to do your best to support that work. Of course, some of those requests are going to come into conflict so collaboration and compromise is going to be necessary, but the more you can foster a "we are in it together"-type atmosphere the easier it will be to negotiate what those compromises are.

Within the orchestra there is an administrative and artistic hierarchy that can help make the Stage Manager's job a little easier as they try to support so many individual artists. As indicated earlier, each section has a principal musician who leads the section. This person had to audition for that specific position and was selected to serve as the artistic leader of the section. It is not a position that is based on seniority, though it is very possible for the principal to also be the most senior member of the section. The auditions are open so it is possible for an outside musician to be hired into this position. In addition to being the artistic leader, they also have a certain number of administrative duties, including deciding who will play what parts in their section and suggesting potential substitute and extra musicians as needed. As a part of their duties, the principals serve as the representative of each section and will provide input on what the overall section needs in order to perform to their best level. This takes the number of individuals the Stage

Manager is negotiating with from over one hundred to maybe seven or eight. You can also use this structure to your advantage in communicating with the orchestra. Certain announcements need to be made to everyone but there are often times, if there is going to be a strange configuration for instance, that you can inform the principals and use that mechanism to communicate the information and field any complaints.

Blurring the lines

One of the very exciting things going on in orchestral music today is a new wave of integrating theatrical elements with traditional classical music. More and more orchestras are trying to push boundaries, and build new and younger audience bases through the use of nontraditional programming. As they do this, there is a push to produce operas and musicals, and even to just add video and lighting to straight-ahead concerts. As with opera companies, the cultural acceptance of classical music as a rich person's art form means that many orchestras are aiming to produce works on a scale that matches this perception, even as they try to make classical music more accessible to all audiences. This competition to produce shows on a larger and larger scale can lead to some really innovative programming that opens opportunities for theatrical Stage Managers to cross into the orchestral world.

It is not common for orchestra Stage Managers to have a theatrical background. They are often former musicians, or even former stagehands, who move into leadership roles in production. This, coupled with their hybrid Stage Manager–Production Manager role means that they often are not able to serve in a traditional, theatrical Stage Manager role when a concert calls for it. If an orchestra is producing a fully staged production of an opera, it is unlikely that the orchestra's Stage Manager will have the required time and skill set to dedicate to being in a rehearsal room, cue artists onto stage, call hundreds of lighting cues, etc. This means that an outside person needs to be hired. These situations are what will allow theatrical Stage Managers to get their feet wet in the orchestral world. It is also what provides an excellent job opportunity for freelance Stage Managers looking to fill a gap in their schedule. Orchestra productions of this nature rarely run longer than a weekend and can provide a well-paid chance to work with a new company with a very limited time commitment. The trade-off is that you will be tag-teaming the show with the orchestra's Stage Manager. They will likely handle everything related to the musicians and the venue. This, in many ways, can make your life easier as you only need focus on the technical running and calling of the show. Because of the soloist/guest conductor nature of the way an orchestral season is programmed, the company very likely already has an infrastructure in place to handle the artist management portion of what you might normally do, so it strips away some of those responsibilities. It is just important to have a conversation with the Producers who hire you to determine what they want your hands in and what they do not.

The single biggest challenge that comes up in crossing over between mediums is the culture shock of the creative teams. Orchestras have a very specific organizational structure that will not change just because they are producing a musical and not an evening of Mozart. As in opera, the conductor has the final say on everything and that can become a point of conflict when working with a director or choreographer who is not aware or not comfortable with that fact. This becomes particularly true when it comes to rehearsal time. Orchestras rehearse for very limited amounts of time for a single program and that does not change just because theatrical elements are being integrated. The difference in the situation between opera and orchestra is that opera conductors are used to sharing their rehearsal time while orchestral conductors are not. This does not mean you are guaranteed problems but as you work with the Director or Choreographer to prepare the show, it is going to be critical that you continue to aim for having the show up and fully functional by the time you get on stage. There will likely not be time to figure things out during an onstage rehearsal with the orchestra so make sure you are evaluating your rehearsal time thoroughly to prepare appropriately. The more you can prepare the show for a plug-and-play scenario, the better.

Working with an orchestra can be an incredibly exciting opportunity but there are challenges along the way. As with any of the disciplines, do what you need to to prepare adequately. This may mean asking the Production Manager if you can attend an orchestra rehearsal or shadow a concert so that you understand what the orchestra is used to. Having that knowledge base can better help you to prepare a cast or creative team for what they will encounter. It will also help you to not be surprised at how things work. For some of these projects you may be hired to be solely a show caller and that can be a ton of fun. However, calling light cues around an orchestra can be stressful because orchestra musicians are not used to having lighting changing around them. Even with stand lights on, if a light cue wash is too saturated or has too much movement, it can become distracting for the players and you will need to manage some of the pushback with the creative team when the orchestra's Stage Manager comes to you and says the cue needs to be changed. The long and short of it is that the more you immerse yourself in the culture of a new discipline, the better off you will be when you have to step into it yourself.

Other music styles

Like classical music, all musical styles will have their own culture you will need to acquaint yourself with. Unlike classical music, other musical styles do not include the same depth of tradition and rules. When it comes to things like rock bands, pop acts, jazz ensembles, etc., you are likely not going to be called a Stage Manager, but will rather hold the title of Production Manager or Tour Manager. When bands move from venue to venue the role of this individual is to work with the venue to ensure that the group has what they need to be able to perform. Whether you are touring a specific show or the band is just taking gigs around the city, country, or world there will be certain accommodations that will need to be made by a presenter that you, as the production representative for the group, will need to ensure are taken care of. These elements are usually included in a rider. Riders are contractual documents that outline the requirements a performer(s) has in order to perform for a presenter. Riders will include hospitality needs, but there is also a section or even a separate document all about production. The notes in a rider provide the presenter with a blueprint for the needs of the artist but every venue is different and changes are made to an act all the time, so it will be the job of the Production/Tour Manager to identify those changes and work with the venue to confirm that everything is ready to go.

Considerations of Production/Tour Manager

- Amplification: The first and foremost issue that comes up with music groups is amplification. Most groups will not travel with their own sound system if they require amplification, and if they did most venues would not allow them to install it. Working with the venue to ensure that their house system will adequately support the artist will fall to the production representative. The band may travel with their own microphones and even their own soundboard, but beyond those items it is likely that it will be the responsibility of the presenter to provide those items. Some bands have a sound engineer who travels with them or functions as a consultant to communicate their needs, but in the absence of that person the Production/Tour Manager will be the one who needs to be able to speak confidently about the band's needs.

- Instruments: Unless it is a very large tour, it is rare that a musical group will travel with all of their own instruments. This is usually due to the size of some of what is required. A string quartet or the like is probably going to bring their own but once you get into the world of percussion, keyboards, electric instruments, and even double basses, you likely will need to source it. Some groups will require a presenter to provide these items and those needs will be outlined in the rider; some will source them themselves, city to city. Which route will depend on the profile of the group, the resources of the presenter, and the specificity that the group may have.

- Lighting: Depending on the type of musical act, lighting can be a major consideration or it can mean nothing. Unless you are touring a major rock or pop act it is unlikely that you will be bringing a lighting designer with you, so the Production/Tour Manager will probably be responsible. The rider may provide some specific items that are required, but more often than not this person will need to walk in the door, see what can be done, and work with the house crew to create a look or multiple lighting states that are appropriate to the show. The world of music pushes Stage Managers more towards the technical than the artistic, but this is one area where their artistic inclinations can shine.

- Furniture and props: Most music groups won't have scenery as a part of their act but they may require tables to lay out instruments, chairs, or stools to perform from; glasses for water, tea, etc.

At the end of the day, the biggest difference between a standing orchestra and a touring music group of any style, is that for a touring group the variability lies in the venues and not the programming. Their Production/Tour Manager will know the music group inside and out and, as with all stage management related positions, it will be that person's job to support the artists so that they can do their best work.

The world of music can be just plain fun. There is such a diversity in the types of music and the artists that one comes into contact with that there truly is never a dull moment. Music also affords Stage Managers the chance to experiment in a unique way from theatre. Assuming you are working with the right orchestra, you can wind up managing a concert with major pop acts, movie stars, or some of the greatest conductors on the planet, and it can all happen in one week of programming. It is a challenging world to work in but, as long as you can roll with the punches, it can be incredibly fulfilling.

9

Role of the Stage Manager: Special Events

Every year, millions of people across the world watch award shows like the Oscars, the Tonys, the Oliviers, and the Grammys on television. You see coverage of the after-parties and the special performances that occur. If you're lucky and influential enough you get invited to attend and see actors, singers, and any number of performers. Each year, the Kennedy Center takes one evening to honor great artists in all fields with a highly visible performance attended by dignitaries, celebrities, and some of the most influential arts makers in the world. Every college and every nonprofit organization hosts galas and fundraisers to bring in funds for special programs or basic operations. Large corporations and major movie studios hold special presentations to show off the new products that they are going to be putting on the market. Each of these varied special events has someone onboard to keep the trains running on time, call the cues, and coordinate the talent so that audiences at home or sitting in the audience get to enjoy a truly special and (hopefully) seamless performance. Management for special events is an incredibly exciting avenue within the overall field of stage management. For those of us who enjoy the rehearsal process and the technical process but then are ready for shows to close after one or two performances, special events provide a great outlet that satisfies those interests.

So what constitutes a special event? What does "special event" mean? Special events are, generally speaking, "one-off" presentations that have a very limited rehearsal time. They usually are directly related to a specific purpose such as raising money or honoring an individual and they tend to be quite exclusive. Stage Managers often take on different titles on special events but the skill set is the same. A great example of this is wedding planning. Every wedding needs somebody to make the event happen the way the bride and groom had hoped it would. It doesn't mean that you need to be the planner for months in advance, you may just be running the day of the event as the coordinator. In that role you would make sure that things run on schedule, interface with vendors, and make sure people walk down the aisle and get on the dance floor at the right time, in the right way. Another great example are donor dinners, which again require coordination if there's some kind of presentation or performance. These performances may be a single singer or a full band, but somebody needs to make sure that the talent is there and ready, they have had a moment to rehearse, the sound checks have happened, and the lighting is correct. Even if the event only features a speaker, the same coordination need apply. The average attendee doesn't think about the dots that a Stage Manager needs to connect to make this all look seamless.

The initial meeting

The first thing to know is that there are no rules when it comes to special events. Special events may as well be built from the ground up every time. Certain events are annual and there is a basic structure that works but, unlike any of the other fields discussed in this text, events have no single culture that you are trying to fit into. The culture depends on the Producer. As a result of all of this it is important that when you are approached about taking on a special event you get the full picture of what to expect. There are a lot of questions that you should try to get answered. Many of these are the same kinds of things that you would want to know if you were working on a theatre show, but often in theatre some topics are taken as assumed because there is a structure; however, this isn't true of events. Below are a number of questions to get clarification on before agreeing to work on a special event.

- Schedule: *What is the expectation for your involvement? Are you just there for the day? Is there a rehearsal process that you're supposed to be managing? What is the prep period like?* These seem like basic things that someone who is hiring you would provide immediately, but it's important that you have your checklist to make sure that you're getting all the answers because you can't take anything for granted when it comes to special events. These shows are often produced by people who do not normally produce live events and as a result you are going to want to clarify as much as you can in advance. Use your knowledge of what it takes to put on a show to help guide the schedule to what you think you would need.

- Staff: *What is the team like?* Different types of special events require different levels of staffing. *Is there a director?* Sometimes on stage activity is "directed" by the Producer and other times the show may as well be a fully staged musical with a full creative team. It is important for you to understand what kind of creative support is being provided. It is also important for you to consider whether you think what is outlined will be adequate.

- The cast: *What is the talent? Who is performing at the show?* As stated earlier, the talent for these kinds of things can be wide and varied. Sometimes you will be looking at a headliner with an opening act and other times it will be a full theatrical cast. Many events include, or contain only, "talking heads." The term "talking heads" refers to speakers, usually behind a podium. Special events tend to come together at the last minute so trying to get a picture of what they are hoping for at the beginning, and then ensuring the Producers keep you in the loop as things develop will help you to better plan for what to expect. Because of their short run they will often attract celebrity guests or people who would not normally have time in their schedules to participate in something that runs longer. Understanding who is confirmed and who is up in the air is also going to be very telling as you decide whether to take the gig or not. The Producer's level of preparedness will help you to assess what kind of event this is going to be so that you can emotionally prepare for what you're getting yourself into.

- The elements: *Is there a creative team? Are there designers associated with this? Will there be a full set or is it just truss and stage? Will there be a lighting designer or is this more an on/off situation that you're going to have to work with the venue to design? If you will be working with an outside lighting company, are you going to be calling the show or is the designer going to be calling?* This is a big one for special events. Practicality may dictate that you will not call all the lighting cues. For one show, it may make more sense for you to call spotlights, since you will be more familiar with the staging, while the LD calls the light cues. Make sure you to have a conversation with the Lighting Designer to be sure you are both on the same page about how you will handle the calling of the show. They may reply that they want to play it by ear or decide once you are in rehearsal, which is fine, but start the conversation early so you can prepare.

- Stage management: *Are you going to get a stage management team?* For some events, you will be hired strictly as a show caller. Show caller means exactly what it sounds like, the person who calls the show. If you are hired in that way you will have no responsibility over the running of the stage and will be strictly tied to the LD and the booth. In those instances, there will be no stage management team and it is likely that the staff from the organization that is producing the event is going to handle the wrangling of talent. Sometimes this makes a huge amount of sense, as in corporate events where the "talent" is high-level administrators. Having representatives from the company be the ones that interface with them and are responsible for getting them to the right places at the right time will be much more efficient. As you get a sense of the scale of the event, make sure you evaluate how many people you think you will require to run it. You, as the Stage Manager, are often going to be the expert in the room on how to pull this off and taking a certain amount of ownership of that is important. Often the folks that are putting on these events are interested in your insight on how best to manage and accomplish what they're trying to achieve. It does not mean you get to become the Director or you take over the conversation, but as you see red flags don't be afraid to point them out. If the event begins to sound progressively more complicated, don't be afraid to ask about getting additional support so that you have the hands you need pull it off.

Getting as much information up front as you can is going to set you up to more effectively manage the event. Don't let the lack of infrastructure corner you in such a way that you're setting yourself up for failure because, ultimately, you only have one shot to get the performance right. The stakes on these shows are very high because, again, they are produced for a very specific reason. If the company is counting on a successful event to generate the funds they need to be able to operate, allowing that event to go down in flames or even stumble becomes a much bigger deal. As the Stage Manager for that event you have to take ownership of that level of risk. You have to be comfortable with the stakes being as high as they are, and you have to have the confidence to know that you can shine in that high-pressure environment.

Making it happen

One of the key differences with working in a special-event environment is that you will find yourself dealing directly with vendors. In a more structured theatrical setting this would be handled by a production manager or other administrative representative from the company. With special events, you will likely have to interface directly and this adds a layer of additional responsibility to the Stage Manager's role. It doesn't mean that you're the one that has sourced equipment or directly booked any of the rental gear, but on the day of the event you will probably have to help direct where things need to be set up based on what has been discussed in the room. You will certainly be working with some other higher-level event coordinator who will handle the larger setup but they will rely on your knowledge of the show for the more detailed elements, like backstage layout, tables and chairs for the cast, dressing room setup, etc.

In most circumstances, you will also serve as the keeper of the schedule. Laying out a very specific schedule of the event day prior to your arrival will create a very helpful road map for all parties. The schedule should be communicated to all departments well in advance so everyone is on the same page of how things will play out. The schedule will shift and change all the way up to the moment you set foot on-site on event day, but having that blueprint is what will keep everyone on track. I often think of the schedules for special events as a to-do list. You have certain concrete times that cannot change, for example when the doors open and when the performance starts, but everything else is flexible. The schedule will provide a checklist to ensure that you have accomplished everything you need to in order to be ready for the event to go on. There will be delays throughout the day and there will be opportunities to catch up, but it will be your responsibility to try to drive the work of the day to accomplish everything that needs to be done by the performance time.

From a purely practical standpoint, wear comfortable clothes during the day. Often, these event will require you to dress in formal wear or business attire. Do not show up the morning of the event dressed for the evening performance. You will regret it and it's not going to do you any favors. Find out in advance if there's a place for you to hang your suit or dress, and if not just leave them in your car. Sneakers and jeans will be your best friends during event days. Show up dressed and ready to run around. Special event management is an incredibly physical job. Events can take place in venues ranging from small ballrooms to major sports arenas, and in all circumstances you will be running around the entire day. It is the nature of the beast. Many of these venues are not equipped with communication tools that are adequate to cover the square footage of the building and, unlike a theatre, you will find events tend to use spaces all over a building rather than being contained to the performance space. You're in a constant state of motion trying to find people, asking questions, providing new information to others, heading off problems, meeting vendors, and guiding folks to the right locations. It's all the confusion and chaos of the first day of rehearsal, first tech, and opening night all rolled into one very busy day.

Event management is also where your patience and flexibility come in handy. All stage management is built around creative problem-solving, but special events, with their tight schedules, take that to the next level. Try to think through potential contingency plans in advance. Try to consider what could possibly go wrong and how you might solve those issues. You will be troubleshooting the entire day of the event so having a few ideas already in your back pocket will help you to keep your cool and roll with whatever comes at you.

When showtime comes hopefully things have gone well during rehearsals and it will run like any other theatrical show. That's the dream but that dream does not always become reality and so, again, flexibility and patience are going to be paramount in your ability to make the performance work. It's really in the active running of the show that the Stage Manager's creativity gets to shine in these kinds of events. When something happens and you need to problem-solve on the fly, there is an incredible adrenaline rush. If you enjoy that challenge and can meet it you will be incredibly successful in the event world.

Events afford you the opportunity to work with people and in venues you may never have thought possible. In this avenue, you could have the opportunity to work with your favorite actors, writers, or athletes, or have the chance to play with technology that, under normal circumstances, a standard production would not be able to afford. Take something like hologram technology, for example. A normal theatre company will never be able to afford to include holograms in a show but a major record label putting together a one-off tribute may be able to find those funds. Working with that kind of technology is fun but it also makes you a more valuable Stage Manager in the market. Stage management is a job you learn by doing and the more experience you can accumulate, the more desirable you are.

Ultimately, special events can be the most fun you will have as a Stage Manager. They can often feel intense but the level of satisfaction and job fulfillment that you feel on the other side is indescribable. If you are given the opportunity to work on an event, you should go for it. If you're not ready to tackle one as the Stage Manager, try to the find a way to assist on one to see what it is like. The question of whether or not to take one of these gigs comes down to the self-assessment issues discussed before. Knowing yourself, your limits, and what you're going to be able to achieve successfully is going to be paramount in deciding whether or not you take it on. It's a challenge you (hopefully) won't regret.

10

Role of the Stage Manager: Theme Parks

It can be said with certainty that if you can stage manage in a theme park then you can stage manage anywhere; the opposite is not always true. Stage managing in a theme park presents an entirely distinct set of challenges and opportunities that you will not find anywhere else. Theme park shows often have much higher budgets than Broadway shows, and incorporate new and exciting technology. This affords Stage Managers an opportunity to call productions that are both challenging and thrilling. Along with the daily shows there are a lot of opportunities for work on special events, these can vary from a red-carpet event for a new movie, a marathon, a press event for the opening of a new attraction, a food and wine festival, the list goes on and on. If you can handle the things thrown at you in a theme park environment you can handle just about anything.

The structure

Theme parks have a lot of the same roles you will find in traditional theatre but the structure is a bit different. Within the theme park environment there is a clear divide between the creative team and the operational team. It is the Stage Manager's job to live at the intersection of those two worlds, which is not always an easy task. Stage Managers need to ensure that the creative team's vision can be developed into a sustainable operation. Keep in mind

The author is most grateful for Kimberly Mitchell's significant contribution to this chapter.

that these shows, once mounted, need to run seven days a week, up to seven times a day.

Below is a list of the key players you will encounter in the theme park entertainment hierarchy:

- Producer: The person responsible for the financial and managerial aspects of mounting a show.
- Show Director (creation): The director responsible for the creation of the show.
- Show Director (maintenance): The director that takes over once the show has opened. This director maintains the show on a regular basis. They usually come to the show once or twice a week to watch and give notes.
- Maintenance Choreographer: The person responsible for the daily maintenance of the artistic integrity of the show. This person is at the show every day and is the eyes and ears of the Show Director when they are not present. The Maintenance Choreographer is also the person responsible for creating the daily deviations (more on daily deviations later).
- Show Maintenance Specialist: The person in charge of maintaining the puppetry in the show. Though the title sounds quite general this role is very specifically focused on puppetry in individual shows.
- Production Manager (reports to the Producer): The person responsible for realizing the visions of the Producer and the Director or Choreographer within constraints of technical and financial possibility.
- Designers: Usually external contractors hired to come in and design the show.
- Production Stage Manager: The person in charge of the overall administration, maintenance, and operation of a show. Including budget, mounting, remounting, rehearsals, liaising with the overall park operations team to ensure that the show runs as a cohesive part of the overall operation of the theme park.
- Calling Stage Manager: Because in theme parks the show runs seven days a week this necessitates a need for more than one Stage Manager to be trained in calling the show. These Stage Managers take on the daily operation of the show but are not responsible for any of the larger administrative and maintenance responsibilities of the show. Those are all taken care of by the Production Stage

Manager. This is not dissimilar to the Deputy Stage Manager role in UK theatre.

- Assistant Stage Manager: Just like a typical ASM these people work the show on a daily basis. They are usually assigned a backstage track (stage right, stage left, etc.) during the show, just like in theatre. However in a theme park, some shows are actually called by ASMs. The shows called by ASMs are usually the ones with smaller casts.
- Technicians: In each area there are Technicians that work the show on a daily basis: Light Board Operator, Spot Operator, Front of House Mixer, Deck Crew, etc.

The theme park world is an inherently corporate environment, so not only do you need to be a great Stage Manager to succeed in a theme park but you also need to be a good corporate employee, leader, administrator, and all-round flexible person. You are in a corporate environment filled with people who are looking at the bottom line and how a nonrevenue-generating department is driving guest flow. So when you are in a stage management role in a corporate environment you have to think about things that would not concern you in a typical theatrical Stage Manager job.

In the case of scheduling the performance times of your shows, you need to consider all the other things happening around you. Is there a band marching past your outdoor venue? If so, that is a sound intrusion, and do you need to adjust show times for either your show or the band's performance? Is there a themed character in your show? If so, you have to make sure that character is not also in another offering in close proximity to your show, because part of the theme park environment is maintaining the illusion that these characters are real, so duplication would not fulfill that goal.

It can often take multiple departments to accomplish a specific task. For example, when building schedules for shows or rehearsals, the phone calls and confirmations for performers are made by a separate department. As a result, a director may request to rehearse in a certain way, but that request is then submitted to someone uninvolved with the show who will then contact the performer. While they do their best to schedule in a way that satisfies the original request that may not be deemed possible. Schedules may need to be reworked several times before you can get everyone you need in the room to accomplish the task for that day. Because of this multilayered, multidepartmental process, you must become an expert at good communication and clear instructions.

By the numbers

In order to run a show seven days a week, three to seven times a day, you can't have just one cast. For example, on a large-scale musical with twenty-six characters in the show, you will actually have a cast of thirty-four on a daily basis. Most of your principal characters will have two sets of performers each day, and you will also have a few swings to swing out each supporting performer for at least one performance a day. The term "swing" will come up often in traditional musical theatre as well. Swings are performers who learn multiple tracks for a show. They essentially serve as understudies for a number of different ensemble or supporting roles, so that if someone were to miss a performance there are a number of people who could possibly step in. This means that if you watch a show two times in one day you will likely not see the exact same cast twice.

With thirty-four people available to fill twenty-six roles, someone must decide which cast member is doing which role in which show. The Maintenance Choreographer is responsible for completing the daily deviations each day. This is a grid of who is performing which role in each show. Keep in mind that of those thirty-four people that you have in that day, each could know more than one role.

Beyond just the cast numbers, every day is different backstage as well. There will never be a day where you have the exact same complement of cast, crew, and management on a show.

To give you a sense of what this looks like, let's assume that the bare minimum number of people a single performance of the show takes to run is:

1 Calling Stage Manager
4 Assistant Stage Managers
1 Maintenance Choreographer
17 Technicians
16 Costumers
6 Hair and Makeup
1 House Manager
36 Performers

In order to keep that same show running seven days a week, up to seven times a day, the theme park will actually employ:

7 Calling Stage Managers
18 Assistant Stage Managers

5 Maintenance Choreographers
42 Technicians
67 Costumers
13 Hair and Makeup
7 House Managers
100 Performers

This leaves an infinite number of possible combinations of people. What it means for a Stage Manager in that theme park is that every day that they come in to call a show they are dealing with a different team. There is no consistency, every day you are working with a new set of people who have their own way of doing things, their own way of communicating, and their own personality. It also results in a situation where whatever issue was faced yesterday that has to be followed up on today, must be handled by a completely different group of people. So, as a Stage Manager, each show you call is different. A different combination of cast means watching for ever-changing actions on stage. A different combination of crew means inconsistent timing and levels of competency. The level of flexibility needed to effectively work in that environment is staggering.

Theme park offerings

Theme park shows can range from a small two-person performance on a ground-level stage, to a fifty-person show for 13,000 audience members. The variety that working in a theme park offers is something that allows Stage Managers to strengthen their skills on many levels, as well as preventing them from getting bored. It also can serve as a training ground for new Stage Managers to be able to develop a wide range of experience working in only one place. The various types of shows offered at theme parks are broken down into a number of categories:

- Atmosphere: These are groups that move around the park and perform in various locations, usually not on a formal stage. They are often bands or interactive groups.
- Stage shows: These are your more typical theatrical productions, generally performed in a formal theater.
- Parades/cavalcades: Parades and cavalcades usually move from one end of the park to the other. They perform in a loop that repeats as they move down the route.

- Spectaculars: These are the big-ticket items at a theme park, they are the wow-factor shows like fireworks, water shows, and the big bang of technology.
- Concerts: Theme parks will periodically host concerts of guest bands that they contract in.
- Events/parties: This is kind of the "everything else" category, it can be just about anything. Service celebrations, press openings, company conventions, trade shows, the list goes on and on.

In a theme park, most shows will run seven days a week and up to seven times a day. This means there is a need for more cast, more crew, more management, more everyone really. For example, on a large-scale musical performance in a major theme park, if you have a twenty-five-person cast on stage during the show, you actually need closer to 100 cast members in order to operate the four shows a day, seven days a week, so the scale of everything is really magnified. Now, of those 100 cast members each could know up to five tracks in a show. This means in rehearsals you would need to run the show many more times than a standard one-cast show in order to get everyone put into their roles. As you might imagine, this makes the scheduling process for these rehearsals incredibly complex, and means that the rehearsal process on these shows is nearly neverending, even after they open.

What makes a theme park different?

While performing arts complexes may contain multiple venues and have shows running simultaneously, they are nothing compared to theme parks. Theme parks house an almost infinite number of performance venues, as the streets themselves are considered fair game. They also play host to thousands of visitors a day. As a result, theme parks are held to very high safety standards, and therefore have a department entirely dedicated to safety practices within entertainment. This is where understanding the creative and operational goals becomes very important. The Stage Manager, in all performing arts disciplines, holds a great deal of responsibility for the safety and well-being of their cast. In the case of theme parks, however, they are answerable to a completely different level of scrutiny when it comes to safety practices. They must exist in a middle ground between a corporate safety structure that is always looking to mitigate risk and an artistic process that is being encouraged to push boundaries in order to attract an audience. Functioning as the principle liaison between these competing interests means that the Stage Managers in theme parks have to have an even higher developed level of diplomatic and communication skills.

The unique nature of performing multiple shows in, what is essentially, a massive performance space with constant audience flow leads to a reliance on a multitude of other departments. Their compliance and efficiency can have major repercussions on your ability to successfully make your shows happen. For example, while calling fireworks, you may have to contact the lead at a ride to make sure their queue is cleared out before you start the show because they are in your fallout zone. Or you may have to call the lead of another attraction to make sure it has stopped running because your use of lasers could affect their attraction. This is in addition to concerns about noise overlap, crowd control, and general safety concerns, which could all impede, or even inhibit, your ability to perform your show. With so much simultaneous activity the domino effect of one thing not happening correctly could be disastrous for the park overall. Outside of the controllable logistics of making the park work, weather is a major wild card with a huge effect on theme park entertainment. There are usually contingencies in place for all sorts of weather situations. Generally, theme parks will have a heat-level system where there are park-wide adjustments that are made at each heat level, along with show specific modifications that are made as each heat level is reached. There are usually procedures in place as well for extreme cold and rain. These procedures can range from modifications to cancellations of shows.

The schedule is one of the hardest things about working in a theme park environment. Most theme parks are open 365 days a year, meaning when others are taking a holiday you are probably working to provide entertainment for those people who have the day off. Also, depending on the time of year, the park may be open late hours so you could work anywhere from 6:00 a.m. to 2:00 a.m. This could be both a blessing and a curse, as it allows for flexibility if you need it but also can be frustrating to have an ever-changing schedule.

Most theme parks are a union environment, so there is always the element of navigating union regulations and contractual agreements as well. That is, of course, similar to working in the theatrical world; however, sometimes you will encounter unions with different rules to learn and theme parks have their own separate contracts, so the rules are specific to each park. For example, the American Guild of Variety Artists (AGVA) is a union that covers the performers in one of the largest theme parks in the world. The AGVA contract states that cast can only work 60 percent of their scheduled shift. So when planning the performance day, you have to consider the length of the show before you can determine how many shows a particular cast member can be in. This 60 percent remains in effect even in the event of delays in a show that are not the fault of the theme park. If a technical problem causes a pause in a performance the Stage Manager will take time postshow to evaluate if any casting changes need to be made to ensure compliance with the 60 percent rule. These kinds of contractual nuances have to constantly be on the brain.

Speaking of show pauses, or mid-show cancellations, these are far more prevalent in a theme park than pretty much anywhere else. "The show must go on" is not a motto theme parks embody very well. Every theme park, and every show, has a different stance on show pauses or mid-show cancellations, but they are certainly more relaxed than Broadway, for example. As Stage Managers, we are trained to "figure it out" and make the show go on, even in the face of some pretty difficult situations. In theme parks, however, the "go-to" is stop the show, fix it, and restart. One of the reasons for this is "character integrity." For example, Disney characters have an "image" that needs to be protected, so if there is anything that happens in the show that may slightly compromise that image, the show is paused while the issue can be sorted out.

One of the biggest adjustments that a Stage Manager needs to make when working in a theme park is in how they think about their show. When working in a Broadway or regional theater the big picture is the performance as that is the main, if not only, event. In a theme park, the show is just one part of a very large picture. Entertainment is one of the cogs in a very large machine, so you really have to adjust how you think. Your one show might not be the big priority in every moment and you have to be okay with that. You still have to keep it as the priority in your mind and do all that you can to make it great, but you have to understand that in the big picture there is a lot more going on. You also have to think about what that show's role is in the big picture as it is not always solely to entertain people. Sometimes it is a tactic to drive people to one side of the park so that you don't have a bottleneck in another area, and sometimes it is to draw guests to a particular attraction or food offering. In theme parks, entertainment is technically a nonrevenue-generating department, but is often the most expensive part to produce. The shows are generally free once you have paid the theme park admission price. So, whether guests go to see shows or not does not affect the bottom line.

A day in the life of a Theme Park Stage Manager

The Calling Stage Manager for the day arrives about two hours before the first show of the day. First, check your email and reach out to the scheduling department to find out if any of your cast or crew has called in sick for the day. If so (this is always so), you work with the scheduling team to ensure that all cast and crew positions are filled for the day. If for some reason you find that one cast position cannot be filled you work with your Maintenance Choreographer to see what changes can be made to the show in order to accommodate the gap. Do you have a contingency that allows for you to be down a dancer? Do you have a dancer substitute that can go in for a singer and lip sync? Can you adjust the show to accommodate? Every show has a different set of contingencies and guidelines. The Maintenance Choreographer then gets to work on the daily deviations. Then the SM will read the show report from the day before, an important task since you were likely not the SM the day before and need to have an idea of how the shows went. You will make note of any information you need to ask any of the other departments about.

About a half hour after you arrive, the Assistant Stage Managers arrive and start to prepare for the day. They will communicate any changes to the daily casting to both hair and makeup and costuming. Since the wigs and costumes for all the cast are not always housed in the physical theater space, sometimes you have to have those teams bring over costumes or wigs from a larger warehouse space. The ASMs will also work on updating the general announcements for your daily meeting with the cast. Around the same time as the ASMs arrive, your tech and costume teams will arrive and will begin their preshow checks. You will then go down to meet with the tech team to discuss any issues, changes, questions, or challenges for the day. Once the tech meeting is over it is back to the office to check the daily deviations and the general announcements. In the midst of all of this it is important to keep checking your emails in case something unforeseen has come up.

About forty-five minutes after you arrive is the cast-call time: they will start to arrive and file into the dressing rooms and green rooms. About five minutes after their call time it is time for the daily meeting with the cast. The ASMs will call all cast to the green room, and you will head down there with the ASMs and Maintenance Choreographer. You will then conduct the morning meeting, giving the cast any pertinent general announcements, and you will give them an update on the day: what does the weather look like, any changes they need to know about, anything special or different going on that day that they need to know about. If there are modifications to the show because of missing cast, the daily meeting is when the Maintenance Choreographer will talk through any adjustments in staging for the day. After the morning meeting you will go over and check in with the costuming and hair and makeup team, make sure they are all set and answer any questions or concerns they may have. Then back up to the office again to check emails and prep the show report.

ASMs will handle warm-ups with the cast and Maintenance Choreographer; they will also manage any fight calls, trick calls, mic checks, etc. that need to happen. About twenty to thirty minutes before the start of the show you will check in with your House Manager, and give them the house. Then it's up to the booth to make time calls and prepare to call the show. Then you will rinse and repeat for however many shows you have that day. Between shows you will be dealing with any issues the cast or crew have as they come up. At the end of the day you will need to complete the show report and send any pertinent info to the Calling Stage Manager for the next day. Before leaving you will need to approve payroll for the cast that day, and about an hour after the last show you get to go home.

As is fairly clear, the world of theme park stage management is dramatically different from anything else that has been addressed in this text. After seeing how dramatically it deviates from any other performing arts profession, the natural question is, "should I do it?"

The answer is yes, if you want to be challenged in ways that typical theatre will not challenge you. There is no better place to work if you want to have the opportunity to work on shows and events that you won't find anywhere else, or want to develop your skills in adaptability and flexibility. There is quite literally no other job that will give you the chance to watch the sunrise over a castle, while also being brought to your breaking point while mounting a show, only to emerge the next morning and be astonished with what you have accomplished. Possibly the most compelling reason is to get to watch the joy on a child's face when they see their favorite characters come to life on stage.

11

Role of the Stage Manager: Cruise Ships

Travelling the world while getting paid is probably the number one reason why people pursue careers on cruise ships. Many will take any job they can just to get the opportunity to see the world for free. As Stage Managers, we have the unique chance to get paid to travel the world while doing a job we truly love. Cruise ships are themselves a melting pot of cultures from around the world and you, as the Stage Manager, get to have a leadership role in that group. Cruise ships tend to attract younger Stage Managers and other theatrical artists, fresh from school. They often have fewer familial ties than their older counterparts and are looking for an adventure and personal growth. The experience of traveling for months on end can provide a cultural awakening for those who are looking for one. They can also be incredibly difficult to endure for those not ready for it. Unlike many of the other opportunities we have discussed, cruise ships require a commitment and dedication that you have to be sure you are truly ready for before signing on.

On any given contract you will be working closely with a team of thirteen to twenty artists and an overall ship's staff of thousands from over seventy different countries. You are signed to work thirteen hours a day and seven days a week. Maritime law requires ten hours of rest split in two breaks in every twenty-four-hour period. Your responsibilities as a leader in that environment will a require a significant level of patience, flexibility, an openness to new ways of doing things, and a sensitivity to many different cultures. You are also going to deal with a variety of new and difficult conflicts given your close proximity to your coworkers for months on end.

The author is most grateful for Kimberly Mitchell's significant contribution to this chapter.

None of this is positive, nor negative, but rather the reality of what working on a ship means.

There are usually three major productions running on a cruise at any given time. These will be performed by the same cast and run by the same crew. Performances are scheduled in a way that allows guests to see every show during the course of the cruise, if they wish. The major shows are usually some sort of musical review. They often have a theme and are designed to appeal to the broadest audience possible. In recent years certain cruise lines have partnered with Broadway producers to present "full," though almost always heavily edited, productions of Broadway musicals onboard their ships. These major productions, produced by the cruise line, are supplemented by a rotating group of outside artists who come onboard one week, or cruise, at a time. In addition to these performances, which occur in the main theater, there are additional smaller productions that take place in bars, lounges, and other locations around the ship. As the Stage Manager you are responsible for all of these, though the smaller shows are likely going to be run by your support staff. These smaller shows can be lounge acts, bands, and even audience competition shows and trivia games.

The production process

There are two primary production models that you will encounter on ships. The first follows the same basic structure as working on a new production of a show for a regional theater. You will be the Stage Manager for your cast from the first rehearsal to the end of your contract. You are in it together and there is limited turnover during the course of your run. For other cruise lines, you may find yourself inheriting an existing show with a cast already up and running. This follows a process similar to a long-running show on Broadway or on tour. You are the new element being introduced to an existing cast and crew and you will see a lot of change and turnover during the course of your contract. Either way, your general responsibilities to the shows on stage remain the same.

Let's start by looking at the ground-up structure. Again, this mirrors what you would encounter if you took a job stage managing a new production of any theatrical show. You will be the Stage Manager for this show and this cast from the first day of rehearsal to the day the contract ends. In the instance of this model, you may be flown to, and housed at, one of the primary rehearsal ports for the cruise line (usually Florida or Los Angeles). There you will rehearse the show with the cast that you will be working with on your contract. Even if the show is something that is already running onboard a ship, you will have some sort of rehearsal period in a room prior to actually getting onboard.

Once onboard the ship, the production schedule is designed to never disrupt entertainment for the guests onboard. The goal is to make sure that there's never a lull in the audience's experience. With cruise ships you have a constant flow of patrons and it's important for them never to feel like the theater is dark or that they're missing out on something that a previous cruise got to experience. This means that the outgoing cast and Stage Manager will be present and continue to perform for your first week onboard. The outgoing team will perform in the evening while yours will tech the show on stage during the day. In addition to rehearsing the mainstage shows during the course of this week, your cast and staff will be mounting all of the ancillary entertainment options as well. Once this handover week is completed the old group will disembark and you will take over full time.

In this model, in addition to your stage management responsibilities you will also serve as the Company Manager. Because your contract timing and length is tied to the incoming cast, you will serve as their primary administrative supervisor for the duration of the contract. The compromise in taking on those responsibilities is that there is usually going to be a technical supervisor who is also onboard the ship, and whose job it is to manage the crew and technical staff related to the entertainment onboard. The technical supervisor will also maintain the production equipment onboard and see that everything is in good working order. The consolidation of roles in this way is due to purely logistical concerns. There is a limited amount of space to house (or "berth") staff on the ship, and as a result they have to try to keep the number of staff restricted.

In the alternate model, your contract is not directly tied to the cast so you are walking into a preexisting show that is fully operational. The only person you have to worry about replacing is your outgoing counterpart and you will not have the same degree of technical rehearsal during the handoff week. There will, of course, be a handoff period as you will be getting trained on the shows and operations of this ship, but it may not be as robust as the previous model. You will also need to get oriented to the cast and crew you will be managing. As a result of your contract not having a direct link to the cast's, you will not have to add company management responsibilities to your plate. Cast members will rotate, taking the role of Company Manager and overseeing each other when their turn comes. Releasing the cast management duties means that you will absorb the responsibilities of the technical supervisor. This will mean serving as the immediate supervisor for the crew and overseeing the maintenance of the equipment onboard. The position becomes a hybrid of a Stage Manager, Production Manager, and Technical Supervisor.

At this point, the two models converge and become consistent. You are going to function as the head of the production department, meaning that you will ultimately be responsible for the successful execution of all entertainment onboard the ship. This means that everything from on-deck welcome parties to mainstage shows to movie nights by the pool, and even the volume of music playing in the hallways of the ship will be under your purview. The size of your crew can range from only two people on small ships to up to eighteen people. You are managing all those technicians who run all of the entertainment on the entire ship, as well as calling shows in the main theater and overseeing the install for the rotating group of guest entertainers mentioned before. As the Stage Manager you are also responsible for maintaining the artistic integrity of the shows onboard, so you will be scheduling brush-up rehearsals and giving notes to ensure everything remains clean and tight. This quality control element is another integral part of your role onboard but is also another avenue for your artistic side to shine through.

There are no ASMs on cruise ships. Your running crew functions as your ASMs and you must rely on them to run the backstage area. You may have to provide more guidance over headset in a cruise environment than you would otherwise. It just depends on the proficiency of your crew and whether you feel confident about allowing them to make decisions backstage in a quick and logical manner. Generally, people are not hired directly into a Stage Manager position. Most people will come in as stage crew and work their way up. Living onboard the ship means that you are always around so there is an opportunity to observe, train, and move up the ranks quickly.

The shows

The mainstage shows onboard a cruise ship function as the headline entertainment. They are generally conceived and produced by the cruise line itself and are normally review-style productions that have some kind of common theme with broad appeal, such as "The Music of Motown" or something similar. From time to time, you will find one that has a loose plotline or is telling some kind of story, but that is not the norm. They will normally run about forty-five to fifty minutes to be able to rotate people through the theater. Due to the number of passengers who are going to want to see the shows they will need to be performed two to three times a night, so keeping the shows short and the patrons flowing through the doors is important.

The main stage shows incorporate Broadway-style scenery, lighting, costumes, and dance. Automation is used heavily onboard as it is often the safest way to securely move scenery when the ship is being bumped around on the sea. Automation is also notoriously finicky, so it can be a bit of a double-edged sword to have to rely on it so completely. Depending on the show, you may be calling all the cues, only spotlight and automation cues, or may simply call the main curtain out and do nothing until it has to come in again. With the inclusion of timecode and the vast variety of talent that is being booked on cruise lines today, the technical complexity of shows is all over the map.

Depending on your itinerary and the cast that you have onboard, you may opt to hold rehearsals during the afternoons to ensure everyone is remaining consistent and safe in the running of the show. Over time, performances can get looser and that can lead to a deterioration of the quality of the show. It can also lead to an unsafe work environment when you have automated scenery and elements of the production not under your control. It will be up to you to decide how necessary these brush-up rehearsals may be, but they are of critical importance just to be sure everyone is on the same page and safe.

The next type of shows are kind of a grab bag. These are the performances that take place in miscellaneous locations around the ship. As the Stage Manager you will oversee the execution of these shows but not necessarily actively run them. They will be covered by your assistant-level staff. Usually, each bar and lounge onboard will have a simple performance space. This may just be large enough to house a small band or could even just be a dance floor. Each venue will have someone from your staff assigned to it and it will be that person's venue to oversee. The performances that go on in these spaces are usually not technically complex and will vary. They can be anything from a band or singer, to a trivia contest, to talent competitions among the passengers. These function as miniature event spaces more than formal theaters. Outside of these formalized performance venues there will be pop-up entertainment through each cruise itinerary. The weather can have a significant impact on these activities, as many ships will put a band or DJ out by the pool or do movies under the stars. Anything the Cruise Director can come up with is fair game in these spaces.

Guest entertainers are the wildcard in the roster of productions onboard a ship. Each ship has a Cruise Director who is responsible for the programming of activities and entertainment for the guests onboard. These Cruise Directors have a certain amount of creative license from the cruise line to put together engaging and varied entertainment options. The three mainstage shows are produced by the cruise line (and/ or agencies or consultants that they contract) and are of substantial technical complexity so cannot be altered. The place where a Cruise Director gets to be creative is in the booking of guest entertainers. These entertainers can be as simple as a standup comic to as complicated as a magic show with props and scenic elements. More and more cruise lines are looking to book interesting and unique talent to bring onboard their ships. Similarly to special events, short engagements onboard a ship can be very appealing to artists who have small windows in their schedule to fill. From classical musicians to magicians, acrobats, and even Broadway stars, entertainment offerings at sea are getting progressively more diverse. Along with this diversity comes unique challenges for the person in the Stage Manager role.

While the Cruise Director gets to select these entertainers, it is the responsibility of the Stage Manager to get the shows up and running. The schedule for getting most of these shows before an audience is very tight. Many will come onboard the ship the same day as their performance and it is only the very complicated shows that are allocated multiple days in the theater for rehearsal. Generally, the Stage Manager and crew will meet with them at about 5:00 p.m. and do a one-hour rehearsal to see what their show is and what their needs are. Immediately following the rehearsal, the crew will have about an hour to program any lighting, automation, or sound elements they need to prior to the audience being let in and the show getting started. This means that the Stage Manager will have barely any time to process what they might need to call for the show. The whole process is very similar to a special event. The presence of these entertainers is what will keep things interesting for everyone onboard. However, the rest of the shows are done on repeat for the three to six months you are on contract.

Following the fast install and tech of these shows, you have a very quick turnaround in the striking of them. Guest entertainers are usually only onboard for one day (or even part of a day). The primary exception to this rule is a more technically complicated show which may stay in residence for a couple of days. It is also possible to have different shows performing in a single night so you may have to strike the guest's setup immediately and get ready to perform one of the mainstage shows right after. Larger shows, such as magic acts, can have residencies that last a whole month. The longer stay will also provide a bit of a reprieve for the crew from having to install new shows constantly. On any given cruise itinerary, you may be looping around to the same ports week after week and so there may be a consistent rotation of the local guest entertainers. This can also help to ease the stress of installing these shows on the fly as you will have the opportunity to build relationships with the artists and have a sense of what to expect when they are going to be onboard.

Other responsibilities

Your most important job outside of your role as Stage Manager is your safety duty. All crew onboard are assigned a safety duty and most Stage Managers are assigned to be first in charge of a muster station. A muster station is a gathering location for all people in the event of an emergency. Passengers are assigned a muster station based on their cabin location and are required to report to that location in the event something were to happen. Muster stations provide a location for people to take shelter from the elements and receive important updates from the staff. They also allow the staff to confirm that all passengers have been accounted for and have the appropriate life jackets for children and adults. Being "first in charge" of a muster station requires you to be formally certified in conflict resolution and crowd crisis management. These are courses that you will take once you are hired. You should not worry about obtaining those certifications in advance. As first in charge, you are responsible for ensuring that you have all passengers who are assigned to your station and to monitor their condition until the emergency has lifted or everyone has been evacuated. This means that in the event of an actual emergency and evacuation you must remain in your muster station until every person, including crew and staff, has left the ship. This means that you will be among the last individuals to evacuate the ship along with the first officer and other senior members of the ship's staff. It is a scary proposition to have to consider, but you have to take on that significant responsibility should you choose to pursue a career on cruise ships.

The experience

While the work may be interesting or not, depending on your tastes, I believe that the single most appealing element of working on ships is the experience you will get out of it. You are signing up to isolate yourself with strangers for months at a time, in foreign lands, onboard a ship. This may be a frightening prospect but can broaden your horizons in incredible ways. Beyond the work experience, you will receive the life experience that cannot be traded for anything. You have the unique opportunity to work with people from across the world and be exposed to their cultures on top of the cultures of the places you are cruising to. You will likely be running the same itinerary for months on end so you will have the chance to get to know the port cities well and may even come to feel like a local as time goes on.

Members of the entertainment department often have the flexibility to get off the ship in ports as you cruise. Most other departments are required to stay onboard, so they will not have the same access to really enjoy the travel aspect of the cruise ship experience. There are rules that govern this free time off the ship, but you should take advantage if you have the chance. One of the major rules that you need to consider as you manage your staff and their free time to disembark is referred to as "in-port manning." For most ships, this means that at any given time 30 percent of the crew must be onboard and there has to be a representative from each department onboard. Be sensitive to your staff and yourself and stagger who is handling this duty to allow all members of the department to have some time off the ship. Do not squander this incredible opportunity to see the world. Take full advantage of everything that working in this particular discipline can offer.

Unfortunately, there are negatives that go hand in hand with the incredible experiences you will have. One of the harsh realities of working on cruise ships is that you are living a disposable lifestyle, both in terms of possessions and people. You are working with thousands of people and hundreds of them will change over every week. There may be relationships that develop and will stand the test of time but realistically, as soon as people disembark you will likely never see them again. You may become friends with people simply out of necessity and proximity, and neither are the greatest foundation for any relationship. Be aware that almost all cruise ships have strict regulations related to cruise patron and staff contact and relationships, as well as staff relationships onboard.

Another challenge of being a Stage Manager is walking the fine line of being friends with those you are managing and being the boss. This is true in all disciples but you are now spending twenty-four hours a day, seven days a week, with these people. You are more likely to develop friendships with your cast and crew than with anyone else on the ship, but it is important to tread lightly. Being confined for long periods of time can breed frustration and conflict. You can also begin to see the more negative parts of others and yourself emerge. If you have any addictions or vices, those will be magnified significantly onboard a ship due to the close quarters and limited activity options. Alcohol is a significant issue onboard and can be a dangerous instigator of bad behavior. The Stage Manager is ultimately responsible for those they manage, so if someone goes off the ship and gets in trouble at 3:00 a.m., the Stage Manager is going to get the phone call. When those calls come, you have to be able to deal with people as their boss and not as their drinking buddy who just didn't happen to go out with them that night.

There are also significant strains on you professionally. You report directly to a Cruise Director and the person in that position can change two to three times over the course of your contract. This instability in your own boss can cause a lot of stress, particularly if you wind up with someone with whom you do not get along. You don't have the luxury of going home or even getting a few days off in order to clear your head to deal with the stress of the job. This feeling of constantly being at work can be amplified dramatically when you don't have a consistent leader above you. It does, however, make you a more resourceful person. It requires you to think outside the box as you only have yourself and your crew to rely on. When something goes awry, you could be at sea for days at a time without access to the comforts of land, and it is up to you and your team to figure out how to keep the shows running. Succeeding in that challenging environment is going to provide a massive sense of accomplishment, and the skills you build in doing it will only serve to make you a viable professional when you return to land.

Hopefully it is clear from this chapter that working on cruise ships may be challenging but is a worthwhile path to consider. If you are the kind of person who enjoys travel and is up for the challenge, the cruise ship life may be the perfect fit for you. There is a fairly high burnout rate among those who go into cruise ship stage management. It can be tough to be away from home for those long stretches of time and there are even maritime laws in place to ensure no one is at sea for too long to protect people from some of the negative effects of prolonged isolation. You are taking on a whole new level of responsibility outside of what you might perceive to be the job of a Stage Manager, but you have the chance to expose yourself to new ways of life and develop relationships that can give you friends and connections all over the world. As in all things, you have to take the good with the bad and carefully evaluate if you are up to this kind of challenge, but don't be afraid to take the leap. Stepping out of your comfort zone and taking on this whole new batch of challenges can reshape you in ways you cannot possibly imagine.

12

Other Avenues For Your Stage Management Skills

Almost every performing arts discipline requires some form of stage management in order to make shows happen. Arguably, the stage management skill set is the single most versatile in the arts. Stage Managers possess a vast array of knowledge about the various art forms they work in, but it is the way that their minds work and their capabilities as leaders that can easily transfer to other professions, both in and out of the arts. One of the harsh realities of stage management is that it is a high-stress profession that requires very long hours and a heavy commitment. The nature of the job can sometimes prevent people from enjoying some of the parts of life that someone with a more traditional job experiences. Maintaining a good work/life balance is hard as a Stage Manager and, as a result, there is a fairly high burnout rate. At some point in many people's careers they will step away from the job for a period of time and perhaps come back to it after recovering a bit. Stage Managers also tend to enjoy a challenge and may simply be interested in trying something new from time to time. They have the experience and the ability to work in almost any field, it is just a matter of seeking out those opportunities.

Dance

Running alongside opera and theatre is dance. Structurally and hierarchically, dance is so similar to these other two disciplines that it makes sense to include it here, as by this time you have a good sense of how the role of the Stage Manager shifts and pivots depending on the art form. As with the others, there is one person at the top, usually the choreographer, who has the artistic vision for the piece, and they are supported by a team of designers who are servicing that vision. One of the unique elements of dance is that a choreographer serves essentially as the playwright as well. As most, but not all, dance does not have a traditional script, the script is the choreography itself. Dance communicates through movement rather than text, because the choreographer's job is to create that movement they are creating the script. Theatre, musical theatre, and opera each have their own individual traditions, and while each feature works from various genres there are certain consistencies to each discipline. Dance, however, is like music. Ballet, jazz, tap, and modern all fall under the singular umbrella of dance and, like music, the artists can specialize but also jump between styles all the time.

This is not to say that the cultures associated with each style of dance are homogenous. On the contrary, each comes with its own individual traditions. For example, ballet is one of the oldest forms of formalized performance dance. There was a time in history when ballet, opera, and music were the three most recognized performing arts. They served the same highly respected audiences and were often paired together. Many operas include a ballet as a featured section of the show. As a result of this parallel trajectory, the traditions of ballet are equally as regimented as, if not more than, opera. As always, there are exceptions to this depending on who you are working with, but generally the same hierarchical structure applies to both. The method of preparing a ballet dancer to perform is very specific and if you stage manage for a ballet company you will need to learn that structure. Each form of dance has its own unique requirements and a Dance Stage Manager needs to have an understanding and respect for each. Some are more relaxed, some are more strict, and sometimes the tone simply comes down to the company, choreographer, or dancers themselves.

Safety is of paramount importance in the dance world. Stage Managers are always going to be keeping an eye out for the safety of their performers, but with dance it takes on new relevance. Dance is an inherently dangerous art form. The degree and types of movement often put the performers at risk of injuring themselves and so the stage manager must be prepared for that. Dancers straddle a very unique line between athlete and artist, and from a practical standpoint the Stage Manager must look at them as athletes. While most Stage Managers will become certified in cardiopulmonary resuscitation (CPR) and have basic first-aid training,

Stage Managers who specialize in dance will take the time to really understand how to treat common injuries and be sure that the supplies necessary for that treatment are available. Most dancers will have their own stockpile of items that they know they need, but it is worth checking with the theater or company that you're working with and talking to the dancers to determine what items you can provide to support them. Along with the treatment of injuries there are preventative protocols in place for dancers to try and avoid injuries in the first place. Warm-ups are the single most important preventative measure that can be taken. Certain styles, such as ballet, require a formal group warm-up while other times dancers will prefer to take care of themselves. Either way, as the schedule comes together, it's important to always keep in mind that the dancers are going to need some time and space to warm-up their bodies. Being mindful of protecting the safety of the cast and being willing to ask them what they need, and expanding your own knowledge is only going to help build trust with the cast and the company.

As a discipline, dance has the unique ability to bring together all the other art forms that have been discussed in this text. In many ways dance is the most adaptable and is able to absorb the best aspects of theatre, opera, music, and even film. Multimedia integration with dance is more and more popular and being able to play with movement and video has become a fascinating area of study. Dance is constantly pushing the boundaries of what can be done on stage, in a different way than any other discipline and it exists at all levels. In a single concert, there can be a piece with the largest set you have ever worked on and then the next piece has nothing on stage. This variety, coupled with the unique challenges it presents, makes dance an avenue well worth exploring for every Stage Manager.

Careers in the theatre

The most obvious place for Stage Managers looking for new career options to begin searching is in the art form they already call home. Moving to another job within theatre, opera, dance, whatever, allows them a degree of familiarity and expertise which transferring to a whole new industry does not. One of the most common career moves for stage managers is taking a position as a *Production Manager*. There is a common misconception that becoming a Production Manager is a promotion. In reality, Production

Managers and Stage Managers simply have different roles to play. Stage Managers, like cast members, are guest artists when they come to work on a show, while Production Managers are usually full-time staff members of a single organization. If a Stage Manager chooses to take a full-time administrative position with a company, this is not necessarily a promotion but rather a change in career path.

Production Managers oversee the technical needs of a show from the inception of the project through to its final execution. They are normally employed full-time by one company, but there is a market for freelance Production Manager work as well. Depending on the size of the company, there may be one Production Manager who oversees all production needs for the company's season, or a team of them who divide the work up. The specific duties of the Production Manager will vary depending on each company's staffing structure. In some situations, the Production Manager will oversee a staff that includes a Technical Director, Master Electrician, Head of Sound, etc., who will be responsible for their respective department's needs. In others, this staff does not exist and the Production Manager will serve as the catchall, working with outside vendors and individual venue staff in the execution of a production. In either structure, the Production Manager serves as the party ultimately responsible for the technical elements of a show.

Generally speaking, the Production Manager will also serve as the direct supervisor for the stage management team. They will be the individual the Stage Manager can rely on to be the administrative face in the process, alongside the producers. Production Managers will also serve as the liaison for communication with the crew in advance of moving into the theater and will generally be responsible for overseeing all logistics associated with that move. Depending on the company, the Production Manager may also take the lead in budgeting the productions and managing those budgets throughout the production process. This can include bidding-out the build of scenery, getting quotes on the rental of equipment, negotiating contracts for production staff, and numerous other tasks. In the same way that a Stage Manager often needs to fill in the gaps for a production team, so too does the Production Manager for a theatre company. Whereas the Stage Manager is a crucial liaison between Producers, Artistic Directors, Music Directors, Conductors, actors, Directors, and others, the Production Manager is a crucial liaison between Producers, Artistic Directors, Designers, crafts persons, and scenery, costume, lights, sound, makeup, special effects, and other production technical personnel. Remember that in professional theaters and opera companies, along with many performers, the Stage Manager is a member of a union and generally has dual allegiances to union guidelines and agreements *and* the producing organization. Production Managers' key allegiances are only to the producing organization and the staff they lead. The similarity in knowledge base and direct correlation in the way the two roles function within their respective work environments is the reason why production management is such a natural alternative career path for Stage Managers to pursue.

Another, not uncommon, avenue that Stage Managers pursue is directing. In many ways, directing makes even more sense as an alternate path for Stage Managers than moving into production management. Stage Managers spend so much time directly interacting with directors, cast members, and designers, that rolling that experience into assuming the central artistic role on a show is logical. This route is, of course, going to most appeal to Stage Managers who self-identify as artists themselves, but over time every Stage Manager is going to develop an extensive knowledge of how to put a show together. Most Stage Managers who ultimately pursue directing, usually have the inclination towards that profession from the beginning. They are often active participants in the artistic process as a show is being mounted and will naturally gravitate towards being a soundboard for the Director.

Stage Managers have the added benefit of being able to pull the positive elements that they observe in various directors they've worked with and build their own style from what they have learned. This is where self-evaluation and careful assessment of how individuals work together can become a major asset for the Stage Manager. By taking the time to carefully watch how cast, creative teams, and producers respond to a given directorial style, one can start to see what works best in what situation. On top of this, in the role of the Stage Manager they must be able to lead a team of these very same people and so are actively developing one of the most critical skills needed to be a director.

The trap that some Stage Managers turned directors fall into, however, is allowing a history of practicality to strip their work of spontaneity. As a Stage Manager, it is natural to serve as the objective observer who can see the logistical problems and inefficiencies in a director's work. In fact, part of the job is to help problem-solve where they can, but that "fix-it" mentality can sometimes blind individuals to the artistic impulses behind those choices. Just as the Stage Manager's job has a great deal of nuance, so too does the director's, and maintaining a healthy amount of respect for that will only serve someone who wants to try their hand at the job in the future. The Stage Manager's inclination towards careful planning and logistical thinking can also help to provide clear direction to those they would work with in this new way. The years of working with various directors who were indecisive or mercurial in their creative choices often prompts them to overcompensate to not repeat what they perceive as errors, and this can lead to producing work that is more refined and well-executed.

It takes a very special person to be a Stage Manager and it takes a very special person to be a director, and not all Stage Managers are going to be up to the challenge. For those who have the talent, however, it can be an incredibly rewarding career possibility to explore. Using their unique perspective to show their team they care and understand and relate to them will only make for a more positive working experience for everyone. The basic principle of getting work based on who you know, applies to directing in the same way it does to stage management. Building a strong reputation as a Stage Manager and then deciding to make this transition can be hard, and everyone who has successfully transitioned has accomplished it in different ways. It is up to individuals to chart their own course and to use the opportunities they are presented with.

Many Stage Managers will also often pursue company management. Similar to Production Management, a transition to company management is an opportunity to step out of a freelance lifestyle and into a more administrative role with a single company. Stage Managers who discover that what they love most about the job is the engagement with the artists will find that the role of company manager allows them to focus on that specific element. They may have an affinity for the technical but it's not what brings them joy, and if caring for and supporting artists is something they are passionate about company management is a wonderful way to parlay their skills into something that also supports the vocation that they enjoy most. Company management allows one to build close relationships with a variety of artists and strip away some of the technical elements of stage management. It often takes you outside of the rehearsal room and provides a very different set of challenges that the stage management skill set is more than adequate to address. The often full-time nature of the position can also be appealing for people looking for a certain amount of financial stability, which freelancing does not provide. Company management is a great place for people with an interest in higher-level administrative jobs to start to dip their toe into contract negotiations and human resources matters, which production management does not involve.

Along the same creative line as directing is producing. Many Stage Managers make the transition into Producers, and even Artistic Directors, when they are ready to shake up their world and try something new. One of the most positive things about this type of move is that a producer who was a Stage Manager will hopefully bring with them a deeper understanding of the practicalities of what it takes to make a show happen. This can make them a great resource to the creative team during early conversations and help improve the management of the technical expectations of a show overall. Many producers come at their role from the perspective of either an Artistic Collaborator or a Financial Manager. Very few Producers have the technical expertise to be able to shepherd projects from a technical perspective, which creates a unique niche for Stage Managers to slip into.

The best way to decide if producing is something you are interested in is to observe the Producers with whom you work. The role of the Producer is to make a show happen, period. There are no limitations or qualifiers associated with that statement when it comes to the Producer. They are ultimately responsible for a show getting on stage. This usually boils down to the fact that they provide or raise the money required. As the keepers of the finances overall, the Producers are immediately placed at the top of the artistic and/or administrative food chain. Different producers approach their position from a unique perspective and it is well worth examining exactly what they are doing. It may seem glamorous on opening night, but the life of the producer is usually filled with complex contract negotiations, intense pressure to fundraise, and a heavy dose of stress and responsibility surrounding the critical and financial success of the production. These are all things that the Stage Manager doesn't have to be as concerned with, but it will become the center of their professional lives if they transition to producing. The job is incredibly rewarding but one must have the dedication, passion, and drive to be successful at it.

Other industries

Moving away from the performing world there are number of other industries where the skills of the Stage Manager could be invaluable. The first step in finding these other opportunities is to begin looking for a few basic elements that theatre shares with other industries.

1   **A product is produced**

At the end of the day, a show in any theatrical discipline amounts to a product that is being created for consumption by an audience. The audience can be large or small, commercial or on the fringe, but the ultimate goal is to get people to buy (or view) the product. The Stage Manager's role is to help efficiently and elegantly bring that product to the audience. They do this through liaising with team members, developing organizational systems, coordinating logistics, and so much more. This same structure directly applies to any industry that produces a product, whether it is a physical item, an event, an ad campaign, a magazine, a fundraising initiative, etc.

2   **A team is collaborating**

One of the fundamental roles of the Stage Manager is to work closely with a large group of artists and manage their collaboration to make a show happen. Any professional path that includes a team of people coming together to achieve a goal is going to be ripe for a Stage Manager's touch. In any collaborative setting, there is going to be one person who emerges as the leader. Sometimes that person is leading artistically and sometimes they are leading logistically. Either scenario is going to be a viable avenue for a Stage Manager but the logistical is certainly going to be the easiest to transition directly to. Looking at yourself as a team leader and not simply as a Stage Manager will open numerous doors that might not be immediately obvious.

3   **Organization and communication are key**

Now this one is certainly much broader than the other two, but it points to the versatility of the Stage Manager's skill set. The reality is that almost every profession is going to require both organization and communication, and being incredibly good at both of those things, as most Stage Managers are, is going to make them that much more valuable in the job market. Being able to provide efficiency and structure to an organization that is struggling without them is going to make you invaluable. It is also important for the Stage Manager to keep these in mind when they might be doing a job that they aren't crazy about. As has been mentioned a number of times, stage management is no different than any other job in the entertainment industry. Gainful employment will ultimately come down to who you know. Before you really know anyone, you may have to work jobs outside the industry that have nothing to do with your interests, but these two general common factors can help to make those jobs more bearable.

Wedding planning and coordination

There is a whole chapter in this book dedicated to the role of the Stage Manager in special events. But outside of the Stage Manager's position, there is a whole world of other incredibly critical jobs in the world of events, the first and foremost being planning. Wedding planning, in particular, is becoming an increasingly popular avenue for Stage Managers to pursue either between jobs, or when they are ready for a change of profession. It's becoming progressively more commonplace for couples to hire a planner and/or a coordinator (if that person is not one and the same) to ensure that their wedding day is perfect. Wedding planning allows Stage Managers to blend their organization and logistical skill set with a creativity that is not always afforded them in the theatre. Wedding coordination is no different than managing any other special event.

The *Wedding Planner* is the person who is responsible for overseeing the entirety of the event. They will meet with the couple to determine the couple's likes and dislikes, color preferences, favorite music and food, special traditions, and anything else that is important for the couple to have included in their special day. The Planner will then take that information away and put together some ideas of how those interests and preferences might be able to be incorporated into a cohesive event. This includes everything from DJ options to centerpieces, flowers to table decorations, and most importantly venues. The Planner is essentially responsible for every element of the wedding that the couples wants them to be responsible for. Some couples will come in with a venue preselected or a specific DJ or caterer they will want to use, so the Planner needs to be flexible enough to run with whatever they are given.

Beyond the decorative components of the wedding, the Planner will also advise the couple on the way a ceremony will run. If it is a religious ceremony, with very strict traditions, this might be easy, but for weddings that follow no predetermined structure, or are combining multiple cultural traditions, this can be complicated. Whereas in the first part of the process the Planner functions almost as the design team would, in this part the Director/Stage Manager side gets to come out.

The basics of a wedding ceremony

1 Preceremony

Before the ceremony begins, the guests need to arrive. Depending on the venue there will be a number of options on how to handle arrivals, and it is up to the couple how they want to do this. Traditionally the groomsmen will act as ushers and help greet and escort people to the appropriate seating areas, but this is not a requirement. It is not uncommon for guests to be greeted by family members of the couple or to even have venue staff direct people. In the UK, there is a tradition of the wedding breakfast or lunch, depending on what time the ceremony begins. In these instances, the guests are greeted and treated to a buffet-style breakfast or lunch and get to mingle for a while, prior to them moving to the seating area for the ceremony itself. Often in these instances the bride and groom will make a brief appearance to greet people, which they are unlikely to do if the guests are heading directly to the ceremony.

2 The aisle

One of the things that is often taken for granted is the procession down the aisle. People think about who will walk with whom and the traditional order (parents first, followed by bridal party, followed by bride), but taking the time to really organize what order the bridal party walks in, where the flower girl and ring bearer may fall in that order, and whether the groom will process or just be preset at the altar are all critically important. On the day, pacing out the speed of people's walks and when each couple starts moving is going to make all the difference to the elegance and refinement of the moment. Beyond getting them down the aisle, people need to know where they are headed at the end of it. It is not uncommon for members of the bride and groom's respective parties to get emotional and forget where they are meant to stand at the end of the procession. Reminding people as you send them down the aisle is always a wise choice. Once they do get to the end ensure they are reminded of how they should be standing. Bridesmaids with flowers should hold their flowers at their belly button, not limp to their side. Groomsmen should have their hands at their sides and not in pockets. Everyone should be standing up straight for the duration of the ceremony and all eyes and toes should follow the bride as she makes her way to the altar.

3 **The officiant and their speech**

With the internet making everything much easier it has become very popular to have friends or family serve as the officiant for weddings, rather than a religious or governmental figure. Whoever is selected to perform the ceremony, it falls to the planner or the coordinator to ensure that they are ready and prepared for the ceremony. They should be supported in the same way a Stage Manager supports the cast. Along this same line, if the couple has decided to perform any religious or symbolic rituals it is the job of the Planner/Coordinator to ensure that all items associated with these are set in their proper places for the ceremony. Some couples opt to light candles, pour sand in a jar, mix colored liquids, link with each other by having the officiant wrap fabric around their hands, or put a large length of rope around their necks. Whatever the action might be, ensuring that all necessary items are accounted for and in place is of paramount importance.

4 **Music**

Music at a wedding is a very traditional element of a ceremony. What pieces are played and whether they are performed live or prerecorded is up to the couple, but it is rare to find a wedding ceremony that does not include music to some degree. Assisting the couple in the selection of the music and ensuring it occurs on cue is one of the most Stage Manager-esque roles that the Planner/Coordinator plays. This may mean pressing play on a computer yourself or coordinating with a DJ or musicians to ensure everyone is up to speed and ready to make it happen.

5 **The getaway**

Once the ceremony is over, the couple needs to leave and it is often the responsibility of the Planner/Coordinator to ensure all elements of that escape are in place. This can mean ensuring that the car that will be picking them up is present and ready outside, making sure the bags of rice or flower petals are ready to be thrown, or doing whatever else needs to be done during the ceremony so that the postceremony moment can go smoothly.

Wedding Planners walk a unique line of both Designer, Production Manager, Stage Manager, and Director all in one. The couple is really the playwright, providing the given circumstances, and asking the Planner to make it all real. A *Wedding Coordinator*, on the other hand, is usually responsible for the execution of those plans on the day of the wedding. Many couples opt to go with a coordinator only, to save costs and to challenge themselves to put the wedding together on their own. This method is very common and often very successful. Being a coordinator is essentially the same as being the Stage Manager for a special event. You are handed the info and asked to run with it. Weddings can be incredibly fun and rewarding to work on, but they are also especially stressful because of their personal significance to the clients with whom you are working. Most special events carry a financial or PR motivation, but weddings are an incredibly important moment in people's lives and treating them with the respect they deserve will make all the difference. Like retail, the customer in a wedding is always right. At the end of the day, it is their day to shine so ensuring that the couple is getting the day they have been dreaming of should be the Wedding Planner's ultimate goal.

Film and television

There was a time when film and TV was only a great option for a limited number of the stage management population. Because that industry was once centralized to only a couple of major cities (Los Angeles and London), there were limited opportunities, even in major cities such as New York. That has all changed in the last twenty years, and more and more cities are becoming hubs for film and TV production. While Los Angeles remains the home to many of the main offices, films and television shows are being shot all over the world. Atlanta, Vancouver, New York, Belfast, and numerous other places have created financial incentives attractive enough to draw major productions to them. This means that Stage Managers in those cities do not need to pack up their lives and move in order to try their hand at this other world.

Ultimately, film and TV are like any other production. There is a writer, director, a team of designers, a crew, and a cast that all need to be wrangled and organized in order to present something to an audience. Unlike theatre, however, this production contains a whole other layer of cameras, audio recording, postproduction, and budgets that no theatre company can match. The Stage Manager role in film and TV is taken by the *1st Assistant Director*. The 1st AD is a hybrid of a Theatrical Stage Manager and an Opera Assistant Director. Their job is to oversee the entire shoot and make sure that everything runs smoothly and as close to on time as possible. They lead a team of ADs that include the 2nd AD, the 2nd 2nd AD, the 3rd AD, and several Production Assistants. Each of these individuals have a specific role to play and areas of the production that they are responsible for. They function just like an ASM, and just like an ASM their responsibilities vary depending on the production that they are working on. Generally, the team of ADs is responsible for all scheduling for film shoots and coordinating with necessary departments and vendors to make those happen. Depending on the size of the production, there may be whole departments dedicated to transportation, catering, location preparation, etc., and so one of the biggest changes that Stage Managers going into this field have to deal with is a much larger team with whom they are liaising.

Once onsite at the shoot the 1st AD actively runs the shoot day. This person coordinates with various department heads to get shots set up and relay the Director's and creative team's wishes to the people who need to know. This communication role is the single most important function that they play. With such a large number of people onsite, failing to communicate effectively and accurately has the potential to throw the train off the tracks. The rest of the AD and PA team will work to support that communication. That may mean being the representative at other locations on the shoot. Even if the active shooting is happening in one place, there are a number of other areas that the production itself has taken over that need to be managed. The central hub for the production is referred to as *base camp*. This is where the production offices are set up, whether they are actual offices or mobile when on location. Base camp serves as the central point of information and contact for everyone on site. There will always be an AD at base camp fielding questions and managing the control center while the 1st AD manages the shoot. The rest of the team may be over by the trailers or dressing rooms, escorting cast to and from set as they are needed, or over at an adjacent location getting it ready for the production to move over when they are ready. Each show and each day requires something different, so flexibility is key, as every day on a film set is rehearsal, tech, and performance, all in one.

One of the biggest struggles that Stage Managers will face, moving from theatrical disciplines to film is the vocabulary. While the skill set may be totally transferrable, the titles and roles of the staff, the equipment, and just the general vernacular is wildly different. This is a very simple example but, in the theatre, the directions "right" and "left" are based on the actors' perspective from the stage looking out at the audience. As a result, the Stage

Manager, who usually sits in the audience area during rehearsal, trains themselves to invert their own perception of directions to make sure "stage right" and "stage left" are correct in all their notes and communication. In film, however, "camera right" and "camera left" are determined by the audience's perspective. This means that it is the actors who need to reverse their perception of which direction is which to understand what they are being asked to do. This appears as a minor difference but is of major importance when one is trying to communicate properly. It can also be quite difficult to retrain your brain when "stage right and left" have become second nature.

Assuming you are up to the challenge, film and TV is a great option to explore. Your experience with live performance can provide a totally new and helpful perspective to a set, especially as live TV specials are becoming more popular and competition shows with theatrical elements are not going away. In making the transition, you can certainly start trying to break into the industry by making cold inquiries, but the reality is that the union structure of film is even more difficult to navigate than theatre. You will not be hired as an AD on any major productions right off the bat, and joining the union can be a lengthy process. The Director's Guild of America represents Assistant Directors for film and they do have a very competitive training program that can streamline this process. That program is really for those who have decided this is the route they want to take and are committed.

For those who just want to try it out, look for smaller films that might need some help. Many colleges have film programs and the students are constantly producing work for classes. It is very common for them to be looking for someone from outside to assist in this capacity, and while you likely won't get paid much (if anything) the experience can help to inform your consideration of film as an option. Another wonderful way to explore film is to sign up with an extras casting agency. There are many of them and the commitment is low. Getting sent out on calls to be a background extra on a show will allow you to make a little money while getting to observe the workings of the set and maybe build a relationship with the ADs.

Project management

The widest field of opportunity associated with the stage management skill set is probably general project management. Almost every industry that produces a product has some kind of Project Manager working on those endeavors. While it's always going to be important and useful for a Project Manager to have a clear understanding of the industry in which they're working, the fundamental skill set of the Stage Manager—organization, people management, scheduling, foreseeing potential problems, and problem-solving—is going to be an asset on every single project that one could possibly work. From toy development to building construction, anything that needs physical production is going to need someone supporting and coordinating all the different people and factors involved in realizing whatever that vision might be.

Outside of industries where something is physically produced, marketing companies, political organizations, foundations, charities, and any number of other organizations are going to require the same kind of project management support for their initiatives. It's very possible that a full-time role as a Project Manager with these companies will not be available, but as a freelancer being able to jump from project to project and company to company to function as that support system would be an ideal way to create a career utilizing the stage management skill set outside of the performing arts.

As an example, politics is a great application of those skills that is often not thought about alongside stage management. Campaign Advisors and Campaign Managers, as well as the lower-level support structure within a political campaign, are going to need to have the same fundamental abilities that a Stage Manager has. A candidate needs people around them that can manage a massive staff, coordinate events, interface with the press, donors, and other personalities, and be able to maintain a fiscally responsible and efficient production. Every level of politics requires those types of people, not just campaigns. Like every professional avenue discussed here there is a significant learning curve, and this is not an area that someone with no interest in the political process can simply step into. However, if an individual has that passion, combining it with the skill set they developed as a Stage Manager could produce a true asset to a political team.

This same explanation can be applied to any number of professions. It really comes down to the personal interests of the individual who is searching for something new. One of the truly great things about the stage management skill set is that it can transfer so easily. While the terminology and the day-to-day grind are very specific, the base skill set is so broadly applicable that Stage Managers can work in almost any field they desire.

In many ways, Stage Managers are the most versatile members of any production. Often Stage Managers feel pigeonholed to stay on a single track. They define themselves as an Opera Stage Manager or a Dance Stage Manager or a Theatre Stage Manager but, at the end of the day, the fundamental skill set is the same. And beyond the performing arts, today's managers can apply that skill set to a multitude of professions. A Stage Manager's only limitation to their professional development is their own imagination. The work that one does in this role will prepare them to step into whatever avenue is of interest. Whether that is the entrepreneurship to build their own company or walking into someone else's organization and helping to organize, develop, and manage things better. Don't ever be afraid to explore other options because a good Stage Manager, a flexible Stage Manager, a well-rounded Stage Manager can do almost anything.

Conclusion

Stage management is not a field for the faint of heart. In all honesty, it is hard. It will never really stop being hard. Some shows will be incredibly fun and fill you with unending joy, and others will make you want to quit daily. As pessimistic as that may sound, it is a truth that every Stage Manager lives with. Despite the stress, anxiety, and exhaustion, they still pick themselves up and sign on for the next gig. They do this, not because they are gluttons for punishment but because they love the job they do. It is a part of them. Often, you will hear actors say things like, "I act because I can't imagine doing anything else." I can guarantee you that every Stage Manager has imagined themselves doing something else, but they keep coming back.

Stage management is a profession that demands a unique level of dedication and commitment, and that is why not everyone can step in to do it. The best Stage Managers are those that find joy in the struggle. They are those that see each new issue not as a debilitating hinderance but, rather, a problem to be solved and a challenge to overcome. There will be days where the cracks will show, and that is okay. If you are meant to do this job those moments will pass and you will be a better Stage Manager for it. There are a thousand different jobs you can do with a Stage Manager's skill set. Some are in the entertainment industry and some are not. Find the one that keeps you coming back.

Further Reading

Shawn DeSouza-Coelho, *Whenever You're Ready: Nora Polley on Life as a Stratford Festival Stage Manager* (Toronto, EWC Press, 2018).

Cary Gillet and Jay Sheehan, *The Production Manager's Toolkit: Successful Production Management in Theatre and Performing Arts* (New York, Routledge, 2016).

Daniel Ionazzi, *The Stage Management Handbook* (Cincinnati, Betterway Books, 1992).

Thomas A. Kelly, *The Back Stage Guide to Stage Management, 3rd Edition: Traditional and New Methods for Running a Show from First Rehearsal to Last Performance* (New York, Back Stage Books, 2009).

Laurie Kincman, *The Stage Manager's Toolkit: Templates and Communication Techniques to Guide Your Theatre Production from First Meeting to Final Performance* (New York, Routledge, 2nd edition, 2017).

Peter Lawrence, *Production Stage Management for Broadway: From Ideas to Opening Night & Beyond* (Los Angeles, Quite Specific Media Group Ltd, 2015).

Scott McCloud, *Understanding Comics: The Invisible Art* (New York, William Morrow & Company, 1994).

Gail Pallin, *Stage Management: The Essential Handbook* (London, Nick Hern Books, 3rd edition, 2017).

Deborah Patz, *Film Production Management 101, 2nd Edition: Management and Coordination in a Digital Age* (San Francisco, Michael Wiese Productions, 2nd edition, 2011).

Lawrence Stern and Jill Gold, *Stage Management* (New York, Routledge, 11th edition, 2017).

Jim Volz, *How to Run a Theater: Creating, Leading and Managing Professional Theatre* (New York and London, Methuen Drama, 2011).

Index